Lit

Pebbles In My Way
...*Finding God's Grace*

ALICE KLIES

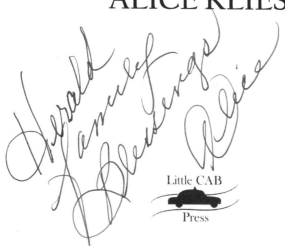

Little CAB
Press

Pebbles In My Way ...Finding God's Grace
By Alice Klies

This publication is a work of fiction based on a memoir of truth. In order to maintain anonymity, in some instances the author has changed the names of individuals and places and may have also changed identifying characteristics and details such as physical properties, occupations and places of residence.

The opinions expressed by authors are not necessarily those of Little CAB Press.

Published by Little CAB Press
www.littlecabpress.com

Published in the United States of America

ISBN: 978-0692946961

I'd like to dedicate this story to all women who lose sight of the fact that God forgives and loves them unconditionally in spite of their shortcomings.

Acknowledgements

Whether or not one believes we need to be still and listen to hear God's voice, it is something I needed to do. I believe God urged me to write a story based on my testimony, a life made up of many poor choices, a life of redemption and finally a realization of how difficult it is to live a Christian life. Most importantly my trials taught me, God is forgiving, trustworthy and almighty. And so… Pebbles In My Way was born.

Thank you first and foremost to my husband, Ray for rescuing me and teaching me about God's grace and allowing me such freedom to be myself.

Thank you to my children, Brett & Stacy Johnston and Lindsey Klies for cheering me on and thank you, Susan Luebke, my daughter-in-law for steadfast encouragement.

A shout out to girlfriends, Dianna Good, Debee Henschen, Nancy Bauer and Suzi Ligget for friendship surpassing the 'norm'.

Without Northern Arizona Word Weavers, I could not have begun this journey in the first place. Thank you for your invaluable critiques, love and prayers.

Thank you Stephanie Bloniarz for your photographic skills and your willingness to love and care for me at the drop of a hat.

Last but not least, a huge thank you to Annette Bonner with Little Cab Press. Her editing, professionalism and her faith in God is a reason for believing in traditional Christian publishers today. Her Godly influence kept me humble and I shall now use the words OH and THAT with much less frequency!!

Chapter One

This morning I feel like I've been traipsing through life with pebbles in my way. You know, the feeling something just isn't right or everything I do seems to end poorly; an irritating something I can't put my finger on. I want to kick the pebbles in my way to get rid of the offending hurt.

Instead, I sit back on a chair in this waiting room. I sweat ripples of fear about what I might hear when I slip through the door I stare at, and walk into my doctor's office. I never perspire, yet besides the dampness forming under my armpits, even the palms of my hands feel wet and sticky. I've always been healthy, but after all I'm forty-two, climbing up the ladder to, what do they say, middle age?

I squirm in my chair. The seat seems harder than I remember feeling on past visits. Perhaps it's just because I threw on such a light pair of jeans when the nurse called.

The days have already turned chilly and my usual attire at home would be my comfy grey sweat pants and hoodie. The nurse asked me to come in as soon as I could.

Wouldn't you know I'd find a chair right in front of a wall clock? I watch the hands tick almost as slowly as molasses drips from its bottle. To the left of the clock, a young man sits with his feet turned inward. He twists his hair with his fingers and bites on his lip. I wonder what he's thinking. Did he come to hear good news or bad news? Maybe he has a simple cold, or worse in my book, an acne problem. His face is rather dotted with mean looking red bumps.

An older woman, who looks to be in her late eighties sits in a wheelchair across from him. She stares into space. It looks like... maybe she has nothing in her thoughts. I feel a little sad. The fiftyish woman sitting next to her might be her caregiver. I hope she's kind to the old woman. I find myself wondering if I'm going to live anywhere near the older woman's age, and if so, what will I be thinking at her stage of life?

Suddenly a red ball rolls between my feet. A blond-headed little girl about seven years old runs across the room toward me. I give the ball a light tap with my foot, sending it rolling back to her. She falls to her knees to catch it in both hands. She looks up at me, wrinkles her nose, giggles, and shoves it back in my direction. I laugh loudly and scoop up the red ball, only this time I bounce it to her. She throws her head back and shrieks.

Now, her mother jumps up from her chair and pulls on the little girl's arm. She scolds her. "Maddie, you are making too much noise." The little girl glances over her shoulder as her mother drags her back to her seat. I blow her a little kiss. She smiles.

I bow my head and think. She's so innocent, this small child, just look at the joy she received from rolling a stupid little ball. I hope her mother doesn't squelch all the child's joyful moments.

I look down and see I'm tapping my toe and don't even realize it. I must really be nervous. What if I have cancer and will never experience a grandchild? I close my eyes and visualize my grown children who have started their own journeys in life. "Karen, the doctor will see you now."

The nurse I've known for years seems distracted. She usually greets me with a big grin. Today she casts her eyes downward and moves to the side of the door. She looks around the room; her eyes sweep it like a police officer looking for a suspect.

Here I go. It doesn't seem real that I have been going through tests all week to determine if I have breast cancer, but here I am. I don't know if the queasy feeling I have in my stomach is fear or the fact I forgot to eat this morning. I usually have breakfast with my boyfriend Jess; always the same thing, a bowl of oatmeal with apple slices and a piece of buttered rye toast.

I'm not married to Jess, but I'm in a beautiful relationship. Will he still care about me if I have to have a breast removed... maybe both? I find it hard to swallow because my throat feels parched. My legs don't seem to want to move so I can stand.

"Karen. Karen, did you hear me?" The nurse taps her pen on the clipboard she holds. She waves a finger toward the open doorway.

"Yes, yes, sorry. Right away." I will my feet and legs to move, but when I stand, a wave of dizziness catches me off guard. I steady myself.

I'm ushered into my doctor's office where most likely I'll wait another thirty minutes. She closes the door. At least she doesn't ask me to put on one of those white gowns dotted with blue polka dots. I'm just here for a consultation. Thank goodness, I don't have to sit up on an exam table where the skimpy white paper usually rips when I move. Whew, just take a deep breath Karen.

The door opens suddenly. My doctor appears and the first thing I notice is his face looks taut. He averts his eyes from mine.

This isn't good. He walks slowly to his desk and sits on his black leather wingchair.

"It's cancer, Karen." His eyes squint into slits before he looks directly at me. "It appears to be stage four. We will do some more tests in order to decide what course of treatment we need to take. I'm so sorry."

"Sorry," I scream. "Sorry is all you have to say?" My fingers ache from the tight grip I plant on the sides of the armchair I sit in. "Am I going to die?"

My hands come off the armchair. They cup around my head at my temples. "How long do I have? Are you serious? Should I pray for a miracle?"

I've known this doctor for ten years. When I look into his eyes, I see he is truly concerned. I move my back deep into the chair to calm my nerves.

"I'm so sorry, Doctor. I'm just so shocked. What am I going to do?"

"I know, Karen, this is very scary to hear; but I can assure you we have so many advanced treatments today that I believe we can beat this." He moves from his chair, walks toward me, and then bends down on one knee. "I've known you a long time. I know your entire family. You have a great support team and we are going to do everything in our power to keep you alive. I've scheduled a few more tests and when we get results, we will begin our battle."

Chapter Two

I feel like my world is crumbling around me. Our battle, my doctor says. Wait, I'm the one who has cancer. Just tell me how this is going to play havoc in his life?

I think he's talking to me right now, but all I can think about is who should I tell first, my Jess or my family? Do I pray for a miracle? I don't listen to my doctor for the next few minutes. I don't hear his last comments. I stand to leave.

I feel numb when I get to my car, put it in gear and head for my apartment. The pebbles I'm stepping over look like boulders.

The route home seems longer. Do I look at everything I pass as a possibility that it might be the last time I view them? I see homes I've driven by for years. I see people out walking their dogs or pushing baby carriages, an activity I witness every night when I make my way home from my office. Why do they seem so important to me now?

By the time I reach my apartment, I have already put myself in a grave. I have listed songs I want played at my funeral and have composed words I hope to have delivered by my children. When I reach the front door of my apartment, I have shoveled the dirt over my casket and I weep openly.

I don't know if Jess is home from work yet. I compose myself before I open the door… just in case. I don't want to cry and feel sorry for myself. My plan is to be valiant and strong.

As I open the door I see Jess sitting on the couch with his feet propped on the coffee table, watching news on the television. He turns toward the door as I walk in and says, "Hi babe, I got home early. How was your day?"

I want to run to the couch and fold myself in his arms. I want to blubber about the fact I have breast cancer and might die soon. I guess my personal strength wins over because I walk calmly to the edge of the couch, scrunch as close as I can to him, and say, "My day was just great honey. I'm glad to be home."

Jess rambles on for several minutes about good news that his music company just picked up some amazing talent, his business looks promising and he has just signed a contract for a new gig with his band.

I snuggle with Jess for a good part of an hour. He's an amazing partner. He has never pressured me about anything. It's pretty rare to have the kind of relationship we have, especially since I'm a divorced mom with two grown children who are already pursuing their dreams. Jess has never married.

When we first started to date, he explained how important his faith is to him. He wants to save himself for a complete union with his wife when he decides to marry. I know this sounds weird by today's worldly views by so many young people, but because he sticks to his word, I have great respect for him. I never question his beliefs. Every time we decide to have a special dinner out, I wonder if he is going to get down on one knee and propose.

I also wonder if I should just blurt out right now that I have been diagnosed with breast cancer, or wait until I know what course of treatment I'll face. I decide to say a little prayer. Maybe God will direct my path. I believe in God, but I really don't know much about His word, you know, the Bible and scripture. I offer up in silence, God, please give me some direction here. What should I do next?

I no sooner finish my prayer, when the volume on the television comes up and a commercial blasts, "Don't wait, get the best treatment possible at Cancer Treatment Center of America."

I doubt God spoke the words in the commercial but I take the message as a sign. I pull back from Jess. "Honey, I saw my doctor today to go over all the tests. You know, the ones I've told you about this past week. Well... he told me today I have stage four cancer."

Jess's entire body stiffens. I feel my eyes mist before they meet his. I'm taken aback by the fear I see in his eyes. Only seconds pass until he grabs me with a fierceness which rattles me. He holds me so tightly I can feel his heart beat.

"Karen I'm so sorry. What can we do? I will be here for you forever. I love you so much."

I knew Jess cared for me, but I'm truly shocked with his outburst and confession of love for me. Neither of us has ever mentioned the love word to each other in all the time we've been together. I tell Jess everything, always, that is on my mind. I consider him my best friend. At this very moment I realize I love him, too.

"Jess, thank you. I love you too. I'm so scared. What if I die?" I fold my body into a ball and lean in to his chest.

He rubs my back. His fingers knead toward my shoulder blades. He tucks my hair behind my ears, and gently pushes me away. His brows knit together. He looks so serious.

"Karen, let's pray right now." He doesn't wait for my reply. He kisses my cheek and closes his eyes. "Heavenly Father, please give us the strength to accept this diagnosis and know, if it be your will, Karen will come through this trial and live to be a witness to others. We thank you for your grace in our lives, Amen." Our heads come together. He plants another kiss on my cheek.

A warm feeling spreads through me which I can't explain. It's not unusual for Jess to pray. He prays before meals and at bedtime. He asks me every Sunday to go to church with him but I always tell him I need to sleep in since I sometimes work on Saturdays. I let this new feeling settle. It feels good.

We decide to have a lite dinner of sliced meat and cheese instead of cooking. Jess tells me, "I'm so sorry I haven't expressed sooner how much you mean to me. I've waited a long time to find someone like you and I want you to know I'll always be by your side to support you in any way possible."

I feel little butterfly tingles in my stomach. Is he going to propose? "I feel the same way. I guess I've felt like I've failed terribly with the marriage scene and just didn't want to admit I might fall in love again." We snuggle, chat about our future together, about our dreams and goals and fall asleep on the couch in each other's arms.

My cell phone's ring wakes us the next morning. My boss's voice booms with excitement. "Karen, I know it's a Saturday, but we just got the go ahead from that client we have been waiting on for months. Is there any way possible you can come in for a few hours today to draw up the contract?"

I rub the corners of my eyes. "Why, yes I suppose I can. Give me about an hour. Okay?"

"Sure, sure, see you soon…and thanks."

I look at Jess, who rolls to his side. "Go ahead, I'll be right here when you get home. We have lots to talk about."

I slip off the couch. I feel a bit crumpled and sore from our sleeping arrangement, but I know a quick shower will fix everything. I kiss Jess on the tip of his nose. "Thank you, I look forward to coming home."

When I arrive at my office, I go directly to my desk to prepare the contract for the new client. A few minutes later, my boss comes into my office. "You are the best to do this for me, Karen. Look for a bonus in your next paycheck." He smiles before he turns to go to his own office.

I complete the contract. I have a few minutes to ponder whether I need to tell my boss about my recent health issue. I also know I have to call my kids and my parents. I'm sure they'll freak out, but right now I think I need to tell my boss. I make my way to his office, knock on the open door and lay the contract on his desk. "Hey Tom, do you have a minute?"

"For you, Karen, any time. What's up?"

"Well," I begin stammering and fiddling with the ends of my hair. "I thought I should tell you I have been diagnosed with breast cancer. I don't have all the details yet, but I feel like you should know."

"Whoa, Karen, I am so sorry." I notice he averts his eyes from mine and looks uncomfortable. Then, his eyes lift, the corners of his mouth turn up and he walks toward me. "Don't worry. We, everyone here at the office, will support you in any way we can. Technology today in treating this kind of cancer is amazing. You will be just fine."

I want to hug him but is it ok to hug my boss? Oh, what the heck! I go ahead and wrap my arms around his neck and whisper, "Thank you."

I make my way back home and my brain is muddled with questions. I can't wait to walk through my apartment door and into Jess's arms. My heart does flip-flops. I smile at myself in the rear view mirror of my car, and repeat, "He loves me," out loud, over and over.

Chapter Three

Well into the evening, Jess and I profess our love, in words, to one another. Just before nine o'clock the doorbell rings. Who can that be? I move from the couch to answer the door. My mother and father stand on the steps and before I register my surprise, they make their way into the apartment and wrap me in hugs.

"Mom, Dad, what are you doing here?" I step back and fiddle with a long strand of my hair, a habit I have when I'm nervous, and one I think I must surely try to conquer.

Jess moves in behind me. "It's my fault. I invited them, Karen. Do come in, Mom and Dad." What's going on, I wonder? Jess moves aside and motions them to sit on the couch.

After they settle in, Jess walks to my dad. He extends his hand, which my dad takes in his. "Mr. Scott, I would like to ask for your daughter's hand in marriage."

Dad stands and pulls his shoulders back. "Jess, I will be honored to have you as a son-in-law." He sits down, puts his arm around my mother's shoulders and gives her a squeeze. I see joy-filled tears pool in my parents' eyes.

I can tell immediately from the emotions I witness, Jess has told my parents about my cancer diagnosis. I rush to the couch and fall at their feet. My own feelings that I've held somewhat at bay begin to flow freely. "Dad, Mom, I'm so scared."

My parents gather me in their arms just like the days when I was a teenager brooding over a romance gone wrong.

"It's going to be alright," my dad says. "Please don't be mad at Jess. He loves you, we love you and any trial is easier when you have a family who fights with you."

Jess sneaks up beside me. He opens his hand to reveal a small velvet box. I gasp when I see it. Jess pulls my left hand to his mouth and kisses the tips of my fingers. "Karen Johnson, will you marry me?"

My arms are outstretched and around his neck before he can snap the lid down on the velvet box. I pull back in order to look directly into his soft blue eyes. "Yes, Jess, yes I will marry you." The same warmth I felt when Jess prayed earlier fills me with hope; hope for a future with this incredible man.

***

The next few days seem to blur together. I call my kids. My daughter works part time in a doctor's office, she hears this kind of story often.

"Have your doctor send me your reports Mom. I will have Dr. Phillip look at them. You are going to be just fine. There are so many new options today. I'll be praying."

One down. I feel pretty good my daughter handled the news so well. I call my son. He's always been more sensitive. He answers the phone. I tell him.

"Really, Mom? So, what are you doing about it? How do you know it's stage four? Maybe you should get another opinion. Do you need me to come there?"

"No, sweetheart. Let's see what the tests say and if I need the surgery we'll think about it. Jess is very supportive and I have Mom and Dad here too."

***

I check into a hospital for more tests, lots of them. When I go for another consultation with my doctor, Jess is at my side. My parents and kids call every day to check on me. My boss and the rest of our staff at my workplace give me high fives every time I'm in the office, and ask to be updated constantly.

The news during this consultation with my doctor gives us great concern. He tells us the cancer might have spread to lymph glands. A few suspicious spots have shown up on my lungs as well. Surgery to remove my breasts will be the first item on the agenda. Chemotherapy will follow immediately. I'm not naïve. I know what to expect. I might lose my hair. I might get very sick. I'm very scared. I want to live. I want to have a future with Jess.

When Jess and I leave the doctor's office and get into the car, he pulls me close. "Let's get married right away Karen." His eyes fill with tears.

"Really, Jess? Is it just because you think I might die?" I lean my head to his chest while I rub at my own tears with the edge of my sleeve.

"No, Karen. I want to be your husband now, for better, for worse. I want to walk by your side forever, till death do we part. I want to be your soul mate." Tears run freely down his cheeks. He pushes them away with a balled up fist. "Please Karen. Let's go to my church tomorrow and see if we can arrange it soon."

"But Jess, I'm not a church goer. Maybe your pastor won't agree to marry us."

"Karen, I know you believe in God. Do you believe that Jesus is God's son and do you believe that He died for our sins and rose to give us eternal life?" He laughs. "Wow, I sound like a preacher, don't I?"

"Yes, Jess, you do, and I do believe. I was raised to believe in these things, but I don't go to church. You've asked me so many times to go with you. I just don't see the need to go to church. I pray to God whenever I want to. Don't you remember? I've told you the only time my family went to church was on Christmas and Easter? I think my mom felt like we could tell people we were Christians because we went on those days." I twist a long strand of my hair.

"Yeah, I do remember; but I think if you would come once, you'd see how great it is to have a church family. My pastor and church will welcome you with open arms. You will meet new family, believers who welcome all who walk through our church doors.

Together we will embrace the love and grace God offers." His chest puffs out like he just proclaimed to be king. "Please, Karen?"

***

Sunday we attend Jess's church. He's certainly right about the welcome his church family offers. Everyone seems to accept me just the way I am. I never met so many people who openly ask if they can pray for my healing. The pastor's message convicts me a little too. I do feel good. Even the thought of surgery isn't as scary for me. I'm not sure I understand this new feeling, which comes over me, but I like it.

After attending a few more Sundays we make an appointment with Pastor Rodney to discuss details of our marriage. He suggests that we attend a marriage counseling session. He also asks me if I have professed my faith in Jesus.

I feel a little stupid asking, but I say, "I guess I don't know what you mean. I believe in God and Jesus for sure. You know, I read children's books when I was little and I know Jesus is God's son. I also attended Catechism classes as a teen. So, is this what you mean?"

"Almost Karen." He moves forward on his chair and takes my hands in his. "In today's world, we use so many clichés that really need some explanation. One of them you may have heard before is, 'asking Jesus into your heart.' Can I ask if you have ever read the Bible?"

"Well no, I mean I know some scripture, you know some of the popular ones like John 3:16." I smile to myself because I see the image of a football player going to his knees and he has this on his forehead.

Pastor Rodney pats my hands. "Yes Karen, that one is well known." He smiles. "An unusual way, I think, for God to bring it to the forefront. So, let's see if I can help you understand. I asked if you had read the Bible because it's so important for us to understand who Christ is, that He is God almighty and God of all creation. Then we have to understand that sin separates us from God. If we are asked to bring Christ into our lives, we need to be faithful to the gospel message."

Pastor Rodney stands and comes in front of his desk to sit on top of it. His facial expression softens.

"You see, Karen, there is so much more to having faith in Christ than just saying we believe. It's a commitment to spend time in God's word, to read scripture and understand His guidelines for our lives. And I might add, this is a constant commitment. Receiving the gift of eternal life by faith is about a trust that God is really in control of our lives. I'm being honest when I say this is really tough in our world today because so many worldly things tempt us." Pastor Rodney reaches to touch my folded hands. "I see by the look on your face I might be overwhelming you?"

I feel a bit uncomfortable as I think about Pastor Rodney's words so far. I'm also fascinated and I think for the first time in my life, I can see professing to be a Christian should not be taken lightly. I adjust my chair to look more directly at Pastor Rodney.

"I admit, Pastor Rodney, I feel a bit stupid. I thought this would be easier; but I want you to know how grateful I am you are taking so much time to help me understand how really hard it is to be able to live a Christ-like life."

"It is hard, Karen, but it's equally important for you to see that it's a process. First, by wanting to change the way your life is going and a genuine desire to confess past sins, big or small is step one. Then to be willing to study a Bible to understand God's guidelines you will see a transformation in your heart. You believe God sent His only son to die for our sins, you just don't know the 'whole story' yet."

I want to stand and hug this man. Instead I ask, "Can I confess my sins now and from this point forward, will you help me?" I look over my shoulder at Jess, who has tears running down his cheeks. A warm fuzzy feeling rushes through me when Jess reaches for my hand and gives it a firm squeeze. My insides melt.

I look at both men. "Is it weird I feel I don't deserve God's absolution, His love that you talk about? I certainly haven't led an angelic life so far and most likely won't in my future."

Pastor Rodney leans back and laughs. "Oh, Karen, we are all sinners. We will never measure up to God's perfect standards, but we can try our best to follow in His footsteps. Your belief in Him, your confession and your desire to read the Bible will bring a smile to His face."

"But, but I've never read a Bible. Do I have to read the whole Bible before we do this? I'm sorry for all the questions, I just want to do the right thing."

I profess my faith to Jesus with the man of my dreams by my side and the warm fuzziness seems to stay with me the rest of the day. I don't feel like the boulders in my shoes are going to stay there forever. I'm feeling some relief and even a bit of hope filters through my brain.

Chapter Four

A week passes and here we stand in front of the automatic doors of our local hospital. Jess holds my left hand and Mom and Dad huddle close by. This is really going to happen.

We walk to the information area, sign in, fill out all the needed paperwork and a nurse ushers us to a room where my vitals will be taken and I'll be prepared for surgery. I feel almost void of emotion. My stomach is a little jittery, but I'm surprised how calm I feel.

Jess leans close and whispers in my ear.

"One step at a time Karen. You've got this." He squeezes my hand tighter. His blue eyes search mine.

I nod. "Yep, I've got this."

I'm prepped for surgery. Jess, Mom and Dad sit on the edge of the bed, and now, a group of our church family surrounds us. They all begin to talk at once. Everyone wishes me a successful surgery and a speedy recovery.

I told my kids to stay put, if I need them after the surgery, we would make arrangements to get them here. I've already been given a low dose sedative. I feel a little loopy. As the nurses push me through the sliding doors to the operating room, I wave and blow kisses.

When I wake up, I look down at my chest. I see my entire chest is wrapped. I feel like a mummy. It looks like there is some kind of drain or tube coming from under the bandages. I don't feel any horrible pain. I want so much to see Jess's face.

Instead my surgeon steps close to my side. "Good afternoon, sleepy head. Surgery went very well, Karen. I can honestly say I don't understand why your lymph nodes don't seem to be affected, but as far as we can tell your cancer seems to be localized. It might have been a stretch to say your cancer was stage four. We will go ahead with chemotherapy but I am really optimistic. Maybe we are looking at some sort of miracle." He leans over and pats my shoulder.

I close my eyes, and then open them raised upward. "Thank you God."

***

Months after my surgery and many chemo treatments, we complete our plans for a simple wedding with friends and family. I call my kids, who make arrangements to arrive on a Friday and leave on a Monday so they don't miss too many workdays.

Our wedding isn't fancy. It seems perfectly normal to me. Doesn't a bride walk down the isle with a shaved head? Doesn't the maid of honor, best man and groom sport shaved heads in honor of the bride?

Debee, my maid of honor, wears a wreath of daisies on her slick head and the groom and best man have dark sunglasses perched on theirs. The day can't possibly be more perfect. I will never forget it.

"I now pronounce you husband and wife." Pastor Rodney puts his hands on our shoulders, gives them a firm squeeze and turns us toward the congregation. "Ladies and gentlemen, I give you Mr. and Mrs. Jess Anderson."

Our reception is held at the church in the Fellowship Hall. My girlfriends have decorated the ceiling with hot pink balloons. The tablecloths are white with the corners tied up in hot pink ribbon. In the center of each table is a shallow black dish with a single pink rose. Jess's band plays all of our favorite songs. We party till midnight, which I begin to feel is more than I'm capable of. Jess sees it too. He takes my hand and motions it's time to leave. We announce our departure, give hugs and kisses to all, and leave.

We race to a limo under a shower of colored Skittles candies. I feel twenty-one all over again.

Once in the limo, I snuggle under Jess's arm. I sleep all the way to our honeymoon suite. I wake long enough to giggle as Jess carries me into the elevator and over the threshold of our room. He lays me in an already turned down bed.

A hard rain belts against our hotel window. The sound wakes me. I look at the clock, which reads eight o'clock. Morning sun peeks through the window. Jess sits on the edge of our bed. He still has his clothes on from the wedding, except he has tossed his jacket over a chair by the window. His hand reaches out to caress my head. His fingers feel slightly rough against my shaved head. "Good morning Mrs. Anderson. I love you." He leans over me. He places his lips just above my eyebrows and lets them travel down the tip of my nose to my mouth.

My heart feels ready to burst. "I love you too Mr. Anderson. Do you think you can undo all these buttons down my back? I'm so sorry I've slept through our wedding night."

As Jess nimbly unbuttons my dress, I'm amazed I don't feel shame about my breast removable. Throughout the entire ordeal, we spoke about my feelings regarding reconstruction surgery, Jess always said the same thing, "God loves you just as you are. I've always been a sucker for qualities of the soul and yours keep me focused on the reason I love you—not your breasts."

My love and best friend brings to a reality that he is mine, and I am his, through a union of gentle lovemaking, which seals our marriage. Exhausted I curl up in his arms for the rest of the morning.

Chapter Five

Treatment has many downsides besides the loss of my hair. Often, I can't eat or when I eat, I promptly empty my tummy. I had to quit work, but my boss is adamant when he tells me as soon as I conquer this, my job waits for me. Jess, my parents, friends and church family cater to my every need. My grown kids call every week. The spots on my lungs turn out to be scars from a case of Valley Fever I contracted years ago when I lived in Arizona.

This is all good news, but the best news is, I've discovered a book which is starting to change my life. I'm also feeling free of those pebbles in my way.

From the time Jess and I married, the Bible has become my choice of reading material. My church family encourages me to just read it from beginning to end, like it's a novel.

"Don't try to decipher every passage, just read it. It's a true story," Pastor Rodney tells me. "Then, you can go back and study individual passages and join a study group."

I can't put the Bible down. I read and read. This evening, I turn the last page of

Revelation. Jess sits next to me. "Wow, Jess. This is like a guide for life." I cover my face with my trembling hands. I peek through my fingers. "Oh Jess, I feel so convicted for so many poor decisions I've made in my forty-two years. I want to go back to my childhood and start over."

I pull my hands apart and look toward the ceiling. I see Jess's eyebrows join on his forehead. The softness in his eyes appears to question me. "I'm so excited Jess, to know how much God loves me. It's hard to believe He forgives me for all the wrongs in my life. I'm beginning to see what a hard task it is to try and imitate God. I have so much to learn."

Jess wraps an arm around my shoulders. "We'll work on doing the best we can Karen... together." He stands and pulls me into his arms. "Now let's get some sleep because we see your doctor early in the morning. Let's say a prayer that all the news we get tomorrow will be good news." Jess lifts me, seemingly without effort, and carries me to our bedroom. I close my eyes and embrace the peace I feel as I listen to Jess's steady voice pray.

***

Here I am again. I sit in the same hard chair I sat in months ago. Only this time, Jess sits next to me with his fingers entwined with mine. The same clock I stared at once before still seems to tick too slowly. I don't see any familiar faces. I wonder if the old woman passed away. If she did, I hope she knew God.

No sign of the little girl with the ball. I sure hope her mom let's her be little for a long time. I see another child, a little boy about two. He still has a pacifier in his little mouth. It seems to comfort him. I can actually hear the smack, smack of his perfectly formed lips as he sucks. I place my hand over Jess's. Will I be so blessed to have grandchildren?

I look at some of the faces in the waiting room, only now I say a silent prayer that whatever the reason they are seeing a doctor, their news will be good and their fate positive.

"Karen... Jess, the doctor will see you now." The nurse's eyes look directly at me. If I didn't know it wasn't proper, I swear she wants to laugh out loud. "Right this way," she motions with an upturned palm. "Turn left at the first door." When I pass her, she winks at me. Hmm, I wonder.

Jess and I settle into wing chairs across from my doctor's desk. Jess stands to shake the doctor's hand when he enters the room. I turn my eyes down and twist my fingers and pick at my nail polish. At least I am not twisting my hair!

My doctor scoots up to sit on the top of his desk. He lets one foot dangle. "You look wonderful Karen. And, I love your smart short hairstyle. Most of all, I love being able to tell you that we cannot find any sign of cancer in your body. The scan is all clear. It's pretty amazing. Sometimes, even we doctors can't find an explanation for what appears to be complete healing. I just call it another miracle. Do you have any questions?"

Jess and I turn toward each other at the same time. His jaw drops several inches and the surprised look on his face makes me giggle. As I jump up to wrap my arms around his neck, he jumps too and my head slams into his nose. His nose starts to spurt blood and we both laugh out loud. I open my purse to grab a tissue and between gulping gasps of laughter, I squeeze Jess's nose together with my fingers.

My doctor runs to one of the patient rooms to retrieve more tissue and Jess and I tumble to the floor. Still laughing, I holler, "It's okay doctor, we have it covered, his nose has almost stopped bleeding." We manage to pull ourselves off the floor, settle back in our chairs and stare at each other in disbelief.

My doctor makes his way back. I look at his pallid face and realize he looks like he has seen a ghost. His lips twitch and break into a wide smile. "I thought we might have to give Jess a blood transfusion."

Now, we all begin to laugh again and fold our arms around our sides.

Jess is the first to speak. "Well, I don't care about the sore nose. The only thing I care about is how grateful I am to hear this amazing news. Thank you Doctor, thank you."

My doctor pushes himself back on to the edge of his desk. "Jess, somehow I don't believe it is me you should be thanking. From all the testing we did, I am truly stunned that we cannot find any signs of cancer in Karen's lymph nodes." His smile grows wider. He points a finger upward. "I think the big guy upstairs may have intervened."

Chapter Six

Jess and I walk hand and hand in silence to our car. Jess opens the car door for me and I lower my head to scoot into my seat. I don't want to let go of his hand. I look up at him. I feel tears forming, bubbling onto my lashes. "Jess, I really believe God heard our prayers. Does this kind of thing happen to other believers? This is just so weird to me. I find myself questioning why God cares about me. How do I thank God?"

Jess looks down, peers deep into my eyes, and bends down on one knee. "Oh, Karen, I too believe God answered our prayers for you to be healed. It's not necessary for us to convince anyone else about this. Our thanks will come through loud and clear by the way we live our lives. God has blessed you with life. Now, let's live it." He stands, and kisses the top of my head.

Funny, now we travel right back down the same roads I traveled when I first got the news of my cancer, once again I look at the people on the street corners. I see some of the mothers with babies, now a year older, some of the same dogs being walked and I feel excitement knowing I will watch them come and go for years to come. Of course, I also realize one day Jess and I will be able to purchase a house, and then we will have new sights to experience.

I walk into the apartment and pull my cell phone out of my pocket. I punch the buttons. I call my son first. When I tell him the good news, I hear him breathing through a long pause. I wonder if he might be crying. But, then his voice is strong with excitement and thanks. Next call is to my daughter. When I tell her, she emphatically tells me doctors don't know everything and she just knew I was going to be fine.

She adds, "Make sure you continue to have checkups with your oncologist." Before I hang up, my phone shows I have an incoming call.

"Mom? Yes, I was just on the phone with the kids. Good news Mom. Jess and I just returned from the doctor's office. I'm free of cancer." My hands shake and I feel my mouth quiver.

After a pause, I think is rather long, I hear my mother sob. "Oh Karen, I am so thrilled to hear this. I can't wait to tell your father. I must call him right away. Can you and Jess come to dinner tonight? We need to celebrate."

"Yes, yes Mom. I'll tell Jess and we can talk about it this evening. I love you."

"I love you too Karen. Till tonight..."

Jess walks up behind me and wraps his arms around my waist. "Was that your mom?"

"Yes. She is beside herself with joy. I've told the kids too and they are thrilled. Mom wants us to come for dinner to celebrate." I snuggle back on to his chest.

Jess nibbles at my ear. "I think maybe we should try to make a baby first."

"What? Really? Not at my age, silly!" I can't contain my own joy as I turn to face him. "I'll race you to the bedroom."

***

We leave the house to have dinner with my parents. The sun has just settled beyond the horizon and the stars threaten to appear. Could life be any more perfect? I lay my head back on the headrest and close my eyes. Jess hums to one of our favorite songs on the radio.

Suddenly he yells. "Whoa Buddy what are you..."

This is all I hear before the sounds of tearing metal screech in my ears. I feel myself being turned upside down. I'm looking up at the floorboard of our car. The continued screech deafens my senses. My fingers dig into the strap of my seat belt. My jaw feels like it flops around without any control to keep it shut. I hear my own voice. I'm screaming "Jess, Jess." Again, and again we seem to flip before a silence settles around me. My seatbelt is tight against my chest. It digs into my neck. My airbag has pushed into my face so only one eye seems to be working. Why am I looking up at the floorboard of our car?

"Jess," I whimper in a whisper. My breath and voice don't seem to want to cooperate with my brain. I try to raise my left hand to wipe at my face. I look down at my fingers. They are covered in red. Blood my brain shouts! I start to scream; my high pitch wail pierces through the still night.

***

Is that a light I see? I try to move, but nothing happens. What's going on? I feel like someone just stabbed me in the heart. I remember. I strain to make my eyes open. Why won't they open? Hello, my mind says. Is anyone here? Where is Jess?

I hear a slight scuffing sound and a voice. "Mr. and Mrs. Scott, I can give you a few minutes with your daughter. She is heavily medicated and in an induced coma, which will help her body heal. We have listed her as critical, but we believe because she is young and strong that she can pull through this."

My mother's voice sounds weak and strained. "Thank you doctor. Can she hear us?"

My mind screams. Yes, I hear you! Can't you hear me? Jess. Where is Jess?

"It is possible, yes, that she can hear us. We don't want to tire her, but I will give you a short time alone with her. It's best not to talk..."

What, what? I'm screaming with all my might. Can't they hear me? Now they are talking so low. What? What? Don't talk about what?

"Sweetheart, Mommy and Daddy are here." Mom's voice sounds strained.

"Yes honey, Mommy and I will be here every day. The kids will be here soon. Everything will be all right. We just have to be patient so you can heal. We love you so much."

Daddy, are you crying? Why are you so sad? Where is Jess? I feel so sleepy. Why do I feel so sleepy? I love you too. Where is Jess? Someone answer me. I feel like I am still screaming.

Chapter Seven

My eyes feel stuck. Ah, there, I see light. Yes, if I can just move my arms. I see a thin strip of light coming through a window with slatted blinds. Where am I? A sharp pain stabs at my temple. Ouch. I feel my brows pull together. I let my eyes turn downward. I'm shocked at what I see. My arms are wrapped in white bandages. My gaze travels to my legs. My right leg hangs from a contraption in the ceiling and it's wrapped too, maybe a cast.

I try my voice. "Hello, is there anyone out there?" I'm a bit raspy. A fog lifts from inside my head. I think I'm in a hospital. I try to move and pain pierces me everywhere. And then... I remember. On no, an accident, I remember the screeching sounds, the tumbling, the blood. Jess, where is Jess? "Help," I think I holler, but the sound is faint, the pain throughout my body now so intense I feel like I'm going to throw up.

A nurse in a crisp white uniform runs into my room. "It's all right Karen. You are okay. You are in the hospital after your car accident. I'm going to get your doctor. Just hold on." She turns and looks back over her shoulder. "I'll get your parents and children too. They're in the hallway."

Tears well in my eyes and I feel like I need to blow my nose. If only I could use my arms. I want Jess. Where is Jess?

My parents and children seem to fly into the room. Close on their heels, I see a rather stout, dark-haired gentleman in white with glasses tipped back on his forehead. My mom holds one hand across her mouth and she reaches the other one out to touch my face. My dad drops down on one knee at the foot of my bed and covers his entire face with his hands. I think he might be crying. My kids flank the side of my bed. Their faces look pale and scared.

The man in white comes directly to the side of my bed. "Hello Karen. I'm Doctor Blake. We thought you might come around and be ready to talk to us today. You have been in a serious car accident. You have multiple bone injuries and some internal damage that is healing nicely. I'm sure your head hurts too, because you have quite a laceration and concussion."

My father butts in. "Oh sweetheart, you are going to be just fine. Mom and I and the kids have been here every day. You are healing so well and..."

I want to shout at all of them. I feel my mouth twist to form the only question I want answered. "Where is Jess?" The effort causes me to cough, which causes more pain than I feel like I can handle. Why won't someone tell me?

The white coated doctor steps back. Mom and Dad come close to my face. They both lay a hand on my chest. My son and daughter grab for my hands. My dad swallows and I see clearly, the pain in his eyes.

"Karen, honey, Jess didn't make it through the car accident. The other car hit your car head on. The driver of the other car didn't make it either. We are so, so sorry."

I watch my mother collapse into my father's arms. My daughter lays her head on the bed and starts to cry. My son squeezes my hand and shakes his head. Did I hear my father right? My Jess is dead? Is that what he just said? My body starts to shake. I don't know what hurts the most, the pain, which wracks my body, or the unbelievable heartbreak, I try to comprehend.

A nurse comes forward. She immediately stands to my side and inserts a needle into my IV. I want to die. I want to scream. I want to thrash my arms and legs. Why God, why? Right now, I think, it's not boulders I need to worry about in my way, it's an avalanche!

When I wake up, I no longer see light. I wonder if I am dead, too. No, I feel so much pain. I must be alive. It must be night. Then

I remember I'm in a hospital. I have survived an accident and Jess, my husband, my true soul mate, is dead. I can't control the tears rolling down my cheeks. I can't control the wails escaping from my throat. I can't control the desire to be dead. Please God, let me die. I can't go on living without Jess.

A small light comes on above my head. A nurse comes quickly to my side. She places her warm hand across my forehead and says. "There, there, little one, you will be okay. Just breathe. I know this is so hard. I'm going to give you a sedative to relax you just enough so your muscles won't tighten so much. You will need to grieve but you need to heal."

Her voice sounds like an angel's voice might sound to soothe a baby. I try to form words from my mouth.

"Why, why," slips out in a whisper before I feel myself drifting away.

I'm awake again, only this time it is light again. I feel less pain and I figure it must be morning. Tears start to form again and my lashes can't contain them as they streak down my cheeks. "Really Karen," I say out loud. "Your tears are not going to change anything. You have to get well." Then I answer myself. "Really? Why should I want to live? I want to die. I want to be with Jess. I hate you, God."

The sweet voiced nurse walks back into my room. "Good morning sunshine. We are going to try some food this morning. I'm going to raise your bed a bit and remove the restraints from your arms." Her eyes twinkle and she winks at me. "Just don't throw anything at me. Okay?"

I feel my lips turn up and a soft chortle comes from my throat. I whisper, "Thank you."

"I know this is not easy, Karen, but you need to start eating. We are going to take your leg out of the trapeze and try to put you into a wheelchair a little later." She walks to my bed and pushes a lever to raise me in a semi-seated position. She reaches under the rail and I feel my arms soften.

I can actually lift my arms. They don't feel like they belong to me, but, I can raise them up and down even though they are stiff in casts. "Here," my nurse says. "I'm going to feed you a little today and later we can work on you feeding yourself. Hope you like chicken and dumplings."

Just as she starts to put a bite of food to my lips, the door opens and my best friend Debee walks in. When I see her, with my mouth full of food I mumble.

"Oh Debee, what am I going to do?" A sliver of dumpling drips down my chin as I reach my casted arms toward her.

She rushes to my side and buries her head in the crook of my neck. We cry for what seems like forever. She pulls away from me and then wipes at her eyes.

"Karen, I am so sorry. I can't even imagine what you are going through."

My nurse moves from the bed, turns slowly and creeps out of the room. Debee pulls one of the side chairs close to my bed and holds my hands in a tight grip.

"We are going to get through this dear friend. I don't know how right this minute. But I do know that I will be here for you always."

Chapter Eight

It seems like I've been in this hospital for my whole life. I'm surprised how fast the time has gone by. My children lost precious time from their work and had to leave. My parents must be exhausted because they visit me every day. I still can't believe I will never see Jess again.

The physical therapy has been awful. I thought I'd never walk again or ever use my arms again for that matter; but here I am, only hours away from being released from this hospital 'prison.' I actually dressed myself. I am only able to put on one shoe and instead of pebbles or boulders, I feel like an entire avalanche has fallen in my way.

Mom and Dad will be here any minute to take care of all the paperwork and off we will go. For a few weeks, I'm going to stay with Mom and Dad; at least until I'm sure I can be mobile enough to be back home in our apartment. Our apartment. I still feel sick when I know how hard it's going to be to walk through the doors of our apartment... Jess's and mine... our apartment.

I squeeze my eyes shut and shake my head. I must not think about this, not yet.

Just as I try to remove my pain from my thoughts, Mom and Dad walk through the door. My dad carries a large bouquet of pink roses, my favorite color since the cancer scare. Of course, it reminds me of the first flowers Jess gave me after he proposed. "Thank you Daddy." I kiss him on his cheek and he hugs me.

"Are you ready sweetheart?" My mom puts her arm around my shoulder and helps me get into a wheelchair. "Paperwork is all done. We just have to wait for an aide to push you out."

My smile comes easy to show my appreciation to my mom. "Thanks Mom. I think I'm ready."

There are lots of goodbye hugs from the hospital staff, who by now are like family. A long stint in a hospital kind of requires such a thing. My angel nurse, the one with such a soothing voice, puts her warm palm against my face. "Don't forget little one, God loves you. He will give you the strength you will need to live again. This I know."

I know she means well. She has been a prayer warrior my entire stay. When she talks like this, I can almost hear Jess's voice telling me the very same things. I don't want to hear any of them. I'm really angry. I want to feel bad. I don't understand how a loving God could take my Jess. I look up. Her dark green eyes bore into mine. I glance down briefly and then nod. "Thank you, Nancy."

In order to get to my parents' home, there is no other route but the one that passes right by our apartment. My parents paid our rent and utilities and Mom kept the place clean during my hospital stay. I asked her to please leave all of Jess's things in the apartment. She argued with me, but I insisted. I'm going to need to smell his shirts, his aftershave, and feel his presence.

The day holds a promise of spring. I notice the trees are peppered with little buds that want to form leaves, which will once again fill branches with life. I push the button on the side of the backseat door to drop the window an inch just so I can breathe in the crisp air. It feels so good. And then, our apartment comes into view. I thought I could do this. "Stop, stop." My hands fly to the window. I push my face close to the glass. "Just let me look at it." I think my heart is going to burst. Oh Jess, how am I going to do this? Tears drip on the scarf around my neck.

Daddy is so patient. He pulls to the side of the road. Then, he reaches through the console to the backseat and grabs my hand.

No words, he just holds my hand. We pause by the apartment for only a few minutes. "Okay Daddy, we can go now. Thank you."

***

Two weeks go by quickly. I'm ready. I'm able to walk with a cane and even though my arms still hurt, I'm able to do most things by myself. I wear a lot of loose clothing and I can even wear regular shoes. My body heals but my heart feels dead.

Mom packs a cooler of food and drinks to take to our apartment. She has made enough dinner meals to last weeks. All I have to do is pop them in the microwave. The drive is uneventful, only three miles away, yet it seems to me it takes forever.

Our landlord stands outside the door of the apartment. When I get close enough to her, she runs toward me with outstretched arms. "Oh Karen, we are so glad you are home. I hope you don't mind I took the liberty to put fresh cut roses in a vase on your kitchen table. I remember how much you love them."

I bring my face next to her cheek. "Thank you, Adele. What a wonderful surprise."

She pushes the door open. I walk in. I so want to see Jess waiting for me. Nothing in the apartment has changed. Just one thing... there is no Jess.

Before I take another step, I turn to see the anguish on my parents' faces.

"Mom, Dad, do you think you can go ahead and leave? I need to do this on my own. Daddy, you can put the cooler in the kitchen. I can put the food away myself. I just need to be alone. I love you both for all you have done and who you are."

Daddy moves to place the cooler in the kitchen and Mom has already hugged me and starts out the door. Daddy pats me on my bottom and says, "Go to it tiger." The door closes with a distinctive click. I melt into the nearest chair and empty my soul with the pent up grief I can now spill out in our own apartment.

Night comes. I lie here in our bed wrapped in Jess's bathrobe, and I breathe in the scent of his aftershave and cry. I rock back and forth. I remember after we married, the first time he and I became one. My gentle Jess, who had remained faithful to God, who had kept his promise of celibacy until he married, brought me to the most fulfilling moment of my life. Now what?

Chapter Nine

I sleep more deep than I expect. A bright morning sun has already skipped past my east window, just far enough to leave a dim piece of sunshine peeking through the shutter. I still have the collar of Jess's robe stuffed close to my nose. I breathe in his smell. I need to get up. Why? I honestly don't know why. My phone rings.

Mom's face pops up on the screen. "Hi Mom." I sit up. Ouch, guess I can't sit up so quickly. I can feel that I'm still mending. "Yes, Mom, I'm doing well. I guess I slept in. Yes, I will be fine. I need this time alone. I hope you understand." I press the end button on my cell.

My phone rings again. My son's picture pops up. "Yes, I'm okay. Is that your sister on the line too?"

"Yes, Mom, it's me. We have you on speaker. I know this is so hard. Please call us if you need to talk. Promise?"

"Yes, yes I will. I'm trying to get settled. I just need some time. I love you both."

It's almost exhausting to get my family to understand I'm okay, even though

I'm not really. Maybe I'll lie here in the bed a little longer.

I wake suddenly. Something must be wrong with the power. It's dark. I look at the clock on my dresser. Oh gosh, it's ten-thirty already. Guess I better have some breakfast. I roll off my bed like the nurse instructed me and feel around for the flashlight Jess always kept by the bed. It dawns on me that even if the lights are off, it should still be light out at ten-thirty. This is when I realize it's ten-thirty at night. I've slept all day. Scripture says that in heaven we will meet our loved ones. Maybe if I lie here forever, I will shrivel up and die and be with Jess again. I bring Jess's robe tighter around my middle and bury my face back into my pillow.

Another morning, more sunshine and the same old me wrapped in Jess's robe. I roll over the edge of my bed to meet the day. Maybe I can't do this. Maybe I need to leave this town; start someplace new, somewhere far away from these memories which haunt me. I slip my feet into Jess's size ten Snoopy slippers. I shuffle into the kitchen. My bad leg doesn't appreciate my shuffling. I wince, and then pull my feet out of the slippers and pad around in my stocking feet.

I pull my phone out of the robe pocket when the shrill tells me someone is calling. There is no ID but I recognize the number.

It's Debee. "Hey girl. Yes, I'm okay. No, it's not easy. I don't know how I can live without him. I know, but it's all so painful. Sure, I will be here. I'll put on a pot of coffee. See you soon."

A half hour later the doorbell rings. "Come on in. The door's open"

I pull two cups from the cupboard, pour the steaming hot coffee and place the cups on the table. Mom has put some sweet rolls on the counter top, so I pull a few out of the package and put them on a plate in the center of the table. Debee comes through the kitchen door and grabs hold of me like she will never let go. It feels so good in her arms. She has been my best friend for a long time. We linger in this embrace. Our tears mingle together and when we pull apart, I hand her a tissue because her black mascara has painted streaks down her cheeks.

For the first time since the accident Debee asks if I want to talk about it. I don't know what to say. Should I talk about it? Will I feel any better if I talk about it? I lay my sweet roll down, twist the ends of my hair... yep, old habit returns.

I look into Debee's stare. "Was it bad? Is the car totaled? Do you know if Jess died immediately? No one talks about the accident. I need to know."

Debee stutters... "Uh, well, well, yes the car was totaled. It was very bad Karen

and yes, the report is that Jess didn't suffer."
She moves sideways on her chair and leans
in closer to me. "It's horrible Karen, all of it.
My heart is broken for you, but you know
Jess is in heaven. He is free of all pain. You
will see him again."

I feel my back stiffen. "What do you
know of pain Debee? You and Bill are
together. You are pregnant and you and Bill
are together. I don't want Jess to be in
heaven. It's not fair. Jess was only forty-
three years old Debee. Forty-three!" I stand
and lean against the sink. I run the hot
water because I can't hold my grief in any
longer. I empty my stomach right there into
the kitchen sink.

Debee is quick to be at my side. She
rubs the back of my neck and whispers. "I'm
so sorry Karen. You are right. I don't know
what it feels like. I'm so sorry. Please know I
will do everything in my power to help you
get through this. Just tell me how I can help
you."

I pull some paper towels from the
holder and blow my nose. Debee wraps her
arms around me and massages my
shoulders. "I don't know how you can help
me Debee. I know I want to be alone. I think
maybe I need to get away for a week or so.
Maybe if I can get away, you can move Jess's
things out of the house. The reminder is
tougher than I thought."

"Karen, of course. But where will you go?"

"I'm not sure. I have an aunt who still lives in Arizona. I'm thinking she might let me stay with her for a few weeks. I love the warm weather Arizona offers. It's actually cooler there in the summer because here in Texas we have this stinking humidity. I might call her later. My mom's sister is widowed. She could be a real help."

I walk Debee to the door. Our hug lasts a long time. "Give me a heads-up when you decide to go. I'll need to get a key from you. I love you Karen. Call me anytime of the day or night. Please?"

"Debee, I will. I promise."

I watch her walk down the steps and up the street. This is when I see her car and my gut tightens. Bill and Jess had purchased the same car, even the same color. They had laughed like two girls when they brought them home. "We're twins" they had boasted. Then they fell down on the couch and laughed hysterically. The lump in my throat feels thick, about to choke me. I back into the house and let the door slam in front of me.

Chapter Ten

The rest of the day, I sit home in a favorite rocker Jess got out of storage. It had belonged to his grandmother. After we married we used to giggle about how we were much too old to think about children, so why do we have a rocking chair? Back and forth I rock. I can't believe I have been sitting here all day. I haven't eaten. Who can eat with so much pain in one's heart?

I look out the living room window. I see night overtaking the day. When I pull myself to an upright position, I feel my leg throb. I need to ask the therapist how long it will be before my pain is completely gone. My arms feel stiff too. I walk to the kitchen to put a kettle on the stove to boil water for tea. Maybe some hot sweet tea will soothe me. I pull Jess's robe tighter around me. Yep, still not dressed.

When the kettle whistles, so does my phone. Mom again. "Hi Mom. I'm fine Mom. Please, I just need some time. Mom, I was wondering, do you think Aunt Mary would let me stay with her a few weeks? I just feel like it might be good for me to get away for a bit. Yes, I'll call her. Thanks Mom, I love you too."

I sit at the kitchen table. Ah, the warmth of the hot teacup feels good against my palms. Well, no time to waste. I dial Aunt Mary's number. "Aunt Mary, it's Karen. I'm doing fair, thank you, but I have a favor to ask. Do you think I could come to Arizona and stay a few weeks with you? Really? Yes, I think it would be good for me too. I'll let you know when I can arrange to come. I love you too."

I have to set the tea down because my hands start to tremble. Am I just running away? There is just so much pain tearing at my heart. Not only because Jess is gone, but the fact I didn't even get to be present when his family buried him. I haven't been able to go to the cemetery because his parents buried him in Oregon. I hardly know his parents. They haven't bothered to call me. Do they think the accident was my fault? Should I call them? I don't even know what to say. Jess had not heard from them in many years. He told me they joined some sort of...what he called a cult.

So, without access to a grave, all I have of Jess is right here in this apartment: clothes, smells, and pictures. I choke on the saliva building in my mouth. Tears don't wait to form on my lashes before they stream down my cheeks. Oh God, why? I bring my knees to my chest and sit in a ball on the kitchen chair.

Is that the doorbell again? Why won't people just leave me alone? I peek out the small window carved into the front door. It's Pastor Rodney from our church. Here I am in Jess' robe, how can I open the door to him? Our church family has been amazing. Not a day went by while I was in the hospital that someone from our church didn't stop by. So, I pull the door open very slowly. "Pastor Rodney, I'm not exactly dressed. Can you give me a few minutes?"

He nods while he tips the corner of his hat. "Sure Karen, I'll just wait here."

Pastor Rodney always wears his brown, kind of Australian backcountry hat. This afternoon, he has it cocked slightly off to one side. I always get one of my warm fuzzy feelings of peace when I'm around him. I hurry to my bedroom and throw on a pair of jeans and a comfy light blue sweatshirt. I take a quick look in the round mirror hanging on the wall. I grab my brush and run it through my still short hair and pinch at my cheeks.

When I open the front door, Pastor Rodney has his hat in his left hand and reaches toward me. The invite is genuine. I fall into his embrace and begin to sob.

"It's going to be okay Karen. Really. I know it doesn't seem possible that anything will ever be okay again, but it will." He holds me tight like a brother might after returning from the military.

I pull back and usher him to the living room. "Please Pastor, sit here on the couch. Can I get you some tea, or coffee?" I wipe my tears away with the back of my hand.

"No, no thank you. I'm fine. How are you really doing Karen? You have been through so much. I want you to know the entire congregation is praying for you. Many of the women have wanted to bring food but your mom told us to wait, you wanted to be alone. No visitors she said."

"Oh, Pastor Rodney, I'm lost. How can any of this be fair? I do appreciate all you and the others have done, but I believe for now, I just need time to sort my feelings. I'm going to visit my aunt in Arizona for a few weeks. As for your prayers, I have to say I'm not very happy with God and I need a break from Him too."

"It's normal Karen for you to feel angry at God. It will most likely be a long time before you will see any good that will come of all this." Pastor Rodney leans over and takes my hand.

I jerk my hand free. "Good? You think this is good? How can you suggest something good will come of this?" I stand, throw my shoulders back and point to the front door.

"Please leave. I don't need you or anyone else to tell me any of this will be okay or good."

Pastor Rodney moves from the couch. I see in his eyes I have reacted too harshly but I don't care. I want him out, now. He pauses and nods again. His voice comes out in almost a whisper.

"I understand Karen. I am truly sorry for your loss. I am available for you to talk to whenever you feel you might need me. You are very much loved and many of us want to help you. In time you will know God is here for you too and He loves you unconditionally." He turns and walks with long strides to let himself out.

I sprawl on the couch, feeling every sore spot in my body trying to heal. My eyes are dry. I pound my fists against the couch pillows before I throw all three of them against the wall. I reach for my phone. "American Airlines, I need a one-way ticket to Phoenix, Arizona tomorrow."

Chapter Eleven

My plane is about to land. I'm lucky the nearly empty flight affords me the pleasure of not having to smile and make small talk with someone sitting in a seat next to me. Aunt Mary will meet me. I haven't seen her in several years but I know she hasn't changed because I keep in contact with her through the good old media.

After Pastor Rodney left yesterday, it only took me a couple hours to pack for this trip to Arizona. I look out the airplane window and the mountain peaks warm my heart. It's so dang flat in Texas! It looks like a sunny day too, not a cloud in the sky. It's April already and I remember when we lived here when I was younger, this is the time of the year in Arizona when the wildflowers start to spring up. This is just what I need... renewal.

I know when I see my aunt she will start to cry. It runs in the family. We are all crybabies. I'm surprised I feel pretty calm, almost like I'm in control, a first for me since the accident. There, I said it... the accident. Look at me, not one drop from my eyes. Well, maybe one teeny little moist ball. I laugh.

Sure enough, Aunt Mary is bawling before I get close enough to hug her. "Karen, Karen, I'm so happy to see you." She can hardly get the words out she is crying so hard.

"And I'm so glad to see you, too, Aunt Mary. You look wonderful. Don't look a day different than when I last saw you at Uncle Joe's memorial." We continue to hold on to each other.

"Let's get your bag. I can't wait to get you settled and catch up on so many years." Aunt May pulls me toward baggage claim.

I've forgotten just how much I love Aunt Mary's home. As we drive up to the large steel gate, it opens automatically when we get close to it. I see the emblem my Uncle Joe made. He was such a John Wayne fan. Right in the center of the gate is a cutout of John Wayne's head. It brings a smile to my face. On each side of the gate, giant Saguaro cacti, each with five and six arms stretching forward, appear to welcome us. My aunt's three dogs come racing to greet us. Big Golden Retrievers, their bushy tails held high in the air, rush at the car and my aunt rolls a window down. "Bubba, Bella, Carlin, shoo, go back to the house." I honestly think they understand English. All three dogs turn and run to sit on the front porch at attention.

I'm already feeling better. I step from the car to a greeting from all three dogs.

Talk about feeling loved. Slurpee kisses bathe my neck and cheeks. "Okay, guys, I love you too." I have to fend myself from more kisses by gently pushing the big lugs to one side. "Oh, Aunt Mary they are so beautiful. I remember Bella and Carlin. Is Bubba the younger one?"

"Yes, we bought him the year before Joe died. Bubba was truly his dog. I think he still misses him. Come on in, let's get you settled." She waves a hand toward the back door of the house. All three dogs follow close behind.

Aunt Mary's house seems to sprawl on forever. The house has an enormous great room with super big windows. The outside view takes my breath away. The Mesquite trees with their lacey looking leaves move ever so slightly in the breeze which has kicked up outside. Then, off in the distance I see Lone Mountain. My heart races a tad because I remember the mountain trails I used to ride my uncle's horses on when I was younger and more recently when I attended Joe's memorial. The purple shadows look like a glaze just poured over the mountaintops to drip and run down the sides.

My aunt's voice brings me back to the moment. "I'm going to let you have the back-bedroom Karen, because you might remember, it has a private entrance to and from the house. This way you can come and go, as you like. The path will take you straight to the barn and arenas. I don't ride much anymore but our wrangler keeps the horses in shape. You're welcome to ride any of them. Your favorite is getting old but he still has some spunk. I keep telling our help Ibn is going to live forever."

I feel like I'm in a fantasy world. I had forgotten how wonderful it feels to put on a pair of boots and kick my heels in the dirt and I can't wait to do it again. As I put my suitcase in the room and look out the window toward the barn I feel sadness and joy. Sad because I remember what a strong gentle man my uncle was. Joy, because memories flood through my head of how much fun I used to have whenever I spent time here.

I look over my shoulder. Aunt Mary is placing clean towels on my bathroom racks. "Aunt Mary, would you mind so much if I changed now and ran out to the barn? I can't wait to put my boots on. I don't even know if they fit. I threw them in my suitcase because I knew I would need them, but it's been a long time since I've had them on my feet."

"You go girl. I'll just clean up a little bit and start some supper. I'll bet Ibn will remember you. You are the only one who could ride him without being bucked off." She let out a belly kind of laugh and blew me a kiss.

This is going to be good, really good. I change into a pair of Levi's and a green sleeveless shirt. The temp outside warrants something light. What did Aunt Mary say? Think she said it's a warm spring already, could mean a hot summer. I bend over to pull my boots on. Whew, they still fit. I wonder if it will hurt my leg to ride? I'll have to be careful. The doctor said everything was healed, but to take it easy. I breathe deeply.

I make my way to the barn. I see Ibn standing alone by one of the water troughs. He looks so majestic. Most Arabians heads appear to have been chiseled out of stone. They are known for the dish between their eyes and the tip of their noses. Their ears are small, pointed and almost touch each other at their tips.

Just as I'm ready to call out to Ibn, he turns, his ears twitch and his nostrils flare. A big whinny bellows from his throat. He starts to run toward me. He stops short of the fence and paws at the ground. He remembers me! Now he starts to run in circles. He bends his head in an arch to the ground. He tosses his white mane from side to side with his tail flagged and waving.

"Yes, Ibn, it's me. You do remember me." I start to run and I surprise myself because my leg doesn't hurt. Look at me, I'm running. Happiness is a new reason for crying. Tears run down my cheeks, my nose drips and I don't care. When I get to the fence, I climb on the rail and throw my arms around Ibn's neck. The soft chortle coming from his throat sounds like heaven in my ear. "I know boy, I've missed you too."

Back in the house, I tell my aunt how Ibn greeted me and how thrilled I am to be here. "Thank you so much for letting me visit. This is just what the doctor ordered."

"I'm so glad Karen. You may stay as long as you want. Believe it or not, I do understand how you are feeling. Joe was taken from me way too soon. Time will heal your heart sweet one, and I have learned many lessons from Joe's passing."

"People keep telling me the same thing Aunt Mary but I can't see anything but the hurt right now."

"I understand, by the way, tomorrow's Sunday. I thought we'd go to the eleven o'clock church service tomorrow. This way you can get a good night's sleep. You remember Pastor David don't you?"

"I do recall hearing of him but I've not met him and I'm not ready for church. I'm having a hard time understanding why God let Jess die. I think I'll go for a ride in the morning if that's okay."

"Suit yourself honey. I'll be back home in time to fix us some lunch." My aunt waves me toward the dinner table. I'm shocked she doesn't try to persuade me to go to church.

Chapter Twelve

My window is on the east side of the house. Sun struggles to seep through the tightly closed shutter. I roll out of bed. I feel only a twinge of discomfort from my leg. I pull on the same pair of jeans from yesterday, wipe at a smudge of dirt and slip a lighter weight sweatshirt on over a clean orange and white shirt. If I layer, I'll be ready for any kind of weather.

As I walk toward the barn, I remember how I used to sit in Ibn's stall for hours the summer he was born. I often fell asleep in the sweet-smelling shavings with my head against his flank. Neither of my children have an interest in the horses. They used to think I was nuts when we visited. Ibn and I formed a bond of some sort. When I rode him the summers I visited I formed a trust with him too and I committed time and energy to him. I muse for a second and say out loud. "Interesting, isn't it, I can feel commitment for a horse, but not my God? Well, at least not now."

I saddle Ibn. I love the strong odor of the soft leather as I strap the cinch around his belly. He puts his head down low and accepts the snaffle bit in his mouth. "Good boy Ibn." I snuggle my face into his neck and rub his throat. I'm glad to see a mounting block against the wall. It will be easier to climb on board with this bum leg.

I'm on. Gosh, this feels so good. I touch the rein against the left side of Ibn's neck and we turn to leave the barn. He is so well trained; a special skill of my uncle's to have done such a good job working with him.

There is nothing quite like seeing the Arizona desert on horseback. I remember when I used to ride with my uncle just as the sun started to rise in the summer, the pink and blue hues seemed to dance over Lone Mountain. Today, the wild flowers I see off to the right by the mesquite trees, bloom in red and yellow. The red poppies are my favorite. Out in front of me, like a blanket covering the dirt, the spring rains have allowed a sea of purple blossoms to put more color on the ground than one can paint on a canvas. I remind myself, I've ridden in the winters as well, when the bareness of the desert brings a different feeling: one of quiet and the ability to see wildlife scurry under bushes no longer holding foliage.

We amble through the trees and brush. I feel alive for the first time in months. I'm a little worried my hind end won't like this too much; it's been so long since I've been on a horse.

Jess would have loved it here. "Oh Ibn, I wish Jess could have known you." Here I go, talking to a horse. There hasn't been a time I've ridden Ibn when I didn't pour my heart out to his pricked-up ears. He never corrects me, shames or blames me for anything. I smile. Ibn actually puts me fifteen hands (his height) closer to God. Now, in this vast desert I scream to the heavens. "God, help me. Why is my Jess gone?"

I realize we have just entered the small canyon I loved as a kid. My words echo back at me. I shudder and feel tingles down my spine. I glance up. A few wisps of white cloud scatter lazily across the sky. "Is that you God?" I ask the echo.

I look down at my watch. Oh gosh, it's almost one o'clock. Aunt Mary will be home from church. "Let's go home Ibn." I give him a light nudge on his side with my heel. He responds and I put him into a gentle trot.

When I get into the house, my aunt has prepared a light lunch. "I'm so sorry I'm late Aunt Mary. I got carried away with my ride."

"No worries, I'm making grilled cheese sandwiches. I remember how you love them. Want some iced tea? Oh, and I have some tomato soup still warm on the stove." She winks at me. "Glad you had a good ride."

She steps from the counter to stir the soup. "Oh, by the way, you had a couple of calls on the house phone. One was your mother. Also, a Debee, and a gentleman who said he was your boss. Oh, and the kids called too. I left the numbers by the phone. I enjoyed visiting with my niece and nephew."

"Sure smells good Aunt Mary, and thanks. I haven't had grilled cheese since college days. Can I dip my sandwich in the tomato soup?" I laugh and step close to her to give her a kiss on her cheek. "Thanks for the messages. I'll call everyone after lunch."

We sit down at the rustic kitchen table, another piece of my uncle's craftsmanship. There didn't seem to be anything he couldn't do. I miss him. I look at my aunt, who nibble on tiny bites of her sandwich. There isn't any sign she is unhappy. How many years has it been? Only five. My Jess has been gone months. I'll never be happy again.

As if my aunt knows my thoughts, she squeezes my forearm. "It will get better Karen. I thought we might go over to Mr. Green's Arabian Farm this afternoon. You saw him at Joe's memorial, don't you remember? It's the big farm at the end of Mulberry. Mr. Green still runs it but his sons do most of the work and have taken over the sales and events.

I'm not exactly 'feeling it,' but I answer as if I am. "Sure, yes, it will be good to see Mr. Green and his sons. Golly, aren't his sons close to my age? What are their names? Kent and James?"

"Well look there, you remember. Yes, I think they are both forty something. Kent's married and has one little boy. His wife Phyllis is a doll. James goes by Jim now. He lost his girlfriend to an aggressive cancer a year ago. Was really sad. We all wonder when, or if, he will ever date again. The boys have been a godsend to me since Joe's passing."

My mouth is full of grilled cheese sandwich, so I just nod. Really, only a year and people wonder about him dating. Not me. Never. Been there done that, twice now! I swallow my food and wipe a bit of cheese from my lips.

Aunt Mary starts to clear the table. I put my hand on her arm. "Let me do the dishes. I'm sure you have chores. I can help with those too, Aunt Mary. Just point me in the right direction and call out orders." I feel my own grin wanting to burst my cheeks. I really do feel better already.

I make return calls to the kids, Mom, Debee and my boss Tom. I assure them I'm doing well and thank them for their concern. Tom called to let me know he will hold my job forever and anything he can do is a given. I step away from the phone and sigh. I return to the kitchen and see Aunt Mary has the dishes already soaking.

I finish the dishes and clean the floors with a Swiffer broom I find leaning against a cupboard. Aunt Mary has gone to the barn to feed some of the animals their medicines. One of the old goats has some sort of respiratory thing. This gives me time to take a quick shower and get cleaned up for our trip to see Mr. Green.

I feel more relaxed and I've only been here a day. I think this is a great decision for me. I pop an antacid in my mouth before I turn the water on for my shower. The grilled cheese must not have agreed with my stomach.

Chapter Thirteen

We start down the very long lane to Mr. Green's red brick home. It's kind of unusual to see the red brick because Arizona homes are mostly stucco. Mr. Green's huge home has been here ever since I was a little girl. The lane is lined with big mulberry trees, also strange for Arizona. The farm is over two hundred acres.

The windows are down on Aunt Mary's truck. The smell is like perfume to my nose. I'm kind of weird this way. I love the smell of horse manure and sawdust shavings. The horses are turned out in the fields. They whinny with a glee of freedom while they gallop in the green pastures. I mentioned before how the Arabians wave their tails like a flag blowing in the wind. Today the field looks like a massive parade with all the flag tails.

Some of the horses lower their heads and flip their manes, while others kick up their heels and squeal as they watch us approach. Newborn fillies and colts snuggle close to their mothers to nurse. Most of the mares draw their heads up to look at us, and then go on about their business munching grass.

Mr. Green stands at the end of the driveway. Guess he expected us. We pull in to a parking area, one usually reserved for clients. Mr. Green puts his thumb out and motions us to a spot. He hasn't aged much at all. I see by the wide grin on his face he is pleased to see me. I jump out before Aunt Mary puts the truck into park.

"Mr. Green, it's so good to see you." He gives me a bear type hug. His grip around my waist is strong as he lifts and spins me around like he thinks I'm still a little girl.

"And you too, you little squirt." He puts me down, pushes me away from his chest and shakes his head. "My, if you aren't a sight for sore eyes, and today, my eyes need a little medicine. Come on in the house. We just finished a late lunch and the boys look forward to seeing you." He grabs my hand and puts his arm around Aunt Mary to guide us toward the house. I smile because Mr. Green still calls his sons boys and he treats me like I'm twelve.

"Look what the cat just hauled in." Mr. Green pushes us in front of himself. Kent first, then James... Jim...leap up from the kitchen table and swoop toward us like eagles catching prey.

Jim speaks first. "Dang, girl, you are looking good. Didn't we see you about five years ago?" He is taller than I remember and quite handsome with dark brown hair, swept off to one side. A day or two old beard shadows his rugged face.

"Let me at her." Kent knocks his brother aside. He holds my shoulders and pushes me away to look deep into my eyes. He stares at me for a few seconds, and then pulls me into a tight embrace. "It's really good to see you, Karen. Come over here, I want you to meet my wife Phyllis and this here is my little boy Jacob."

I look into the most beautiful grey eyes I've ever seen. Phyllis stands and reaches to give me a hardy hug before she bends over to pull a toe-headed little boy out of a booster seat at the table. Jacob looks to be about three. He has his mother's eyes, round and wide and grey. It looks like he's been eating spaghetti since the entire circle around his mouth is a pinkish red.

Phyllis smiles and puts him back in his spot at the table. "You probably don't remember me Karen, but I used to come to your uncle's farm with my father. I met you once. Do you remember the pig tailed little girl who splashed mud all over your church clothes one Sunday?" She giggled and put her hand on her hips.

"Gosh Phyllis, I do remember. There was a big rain puddle right in front of the church and you ran out the church door and took a giant jump right into it with both feet. I was just the innocent bystander. I remember I wanted to join you, but your daddy rescued you. He didn't scold you. He just picked you out of the puddle and laughed, I thought it was so wonderful of him!"

We sit for more than an hour at the kitchen table and reminisce about past visits. I like this. Mr. Green stands and asks, "Karen, would you like to take a spin through the barns? We've made a lot of changes since you were last here."

"Yes, Mr. Green, I'd love to."

***

We stop at the breeding area first. I don't know why, in the past, I didn't get to see this area, but I'm fascinated now. A crisp odor wafts past my nose, a clean antiseptic smell. The tile under my boots shines like a hospital floor. Every cabinet and drawer is neatly marked for content. I see how easy it is for the attendants to find meds. A young man is busy putting supplements and meds into small buckets. I assume he readies them for the horses that need them.

I've forgotten how the barns seem to go on and on in rows. Everything is so clean. Ah, I smell the fresh wood shavings. The fragrance of fresh cut Bermuda hay fills my nose. Mr. Green is very patriotic and red, white and blue halters hang on the front of each stall. Every stall sports a gold plate with the horse's name on it, along with its pedigree.

The last place Mr. Green shows me is the new Sales Center he recently had built. I feel like I'm in a movie set. I see an enormous stage where, during sales, the horses are paraded for clients to view and bid on. Gold curtains flank both sides of the stage. Large television screens are anchored closer to the ceiling. More red, white and blue accessories finish off the patriotic look Mr. Green prides himself with.

We end up back at the front entrance to the main house. "Thank you so much for the tour. I love everything you've done. The farm is beautiful. Is the Arabian Horse business still flourishing?"

Mr. Green puckers his lips. "Well, girl, certainly not like it was in the eighties, but we do fairly well. We are still one of the largest breeders and our horses' bloodlines have maintained their importance. Since the All Arabian Horse Show is still here in Scottsdale, we keep busy showing and selling. I'm actually looking for someone to help me market the horses. Thought maybe you might consider the job."

Did I just hear him offer me a job? I feel a jolt up my back. "Well, I, I, don't know what to say. I'm just here to visit for a short while." I brought a hand to my heart. "Really, Mr. Green, I thank you for such an offer, but I'm reeling from surprise."

"Hey, girl, I know. I didn't mean to spring it on you, but when Mary told me you were coming, I was excited. I know you've been through a real tough time. Just think about it. I'm not in a big hurry. Our big sales season isn't until next February and we don't really start sales previews till September. Just think about it. I could give you lodging as well." He patted my shoulder, took hold of my hands and gave them a strong squeeze. "Keep in touch and while you are here, come see us often, you hear?"

Chapter Fourteen

Aunt Mary and I get back to her house just before the sun starts to hide behind Lone Mountain. "Karen, do you want to check on the animals? I know Charlie, my foreman has already fed and watered; but I usually do a last check just before dark. I'll warm us up some chili. I'm also going to make a Quiche for breakfast so we can warm it before I leave for my stint at the public library."

"On it, Aunt Mary." I hustle out the back door of the kitchen, grateful to have a few minutes to myself to digest Mr. Green's offer. I run my hand over the top of the pipe fences of the pastures. Really, a job here in Arizona... I'd have to let Tom know. I wonder how my parents and close friends will take the news, much less the kids in California? It could be a new beginning for me. Old memories could be put aside.

I get to the main barn to check on the brood mares when I feel that same queasy feeling in my gut. Hmm, I wonder if chili is a good choice for tonight. I check all the stall doors and open the big barrel at the end of the row. I pull out a bunch of carrots. Aunt Mary always gives the stallions in the main barn a special treat in the evening. As I hand each stallion a carrot, I have a hard time thinking about anything but Mr. Green's offer.

By the time I get back to the house, I feel like I might get sick. Maybe I just have a touch of flu coming on. I no sooner get into the kitchen than I run to the bathroom and empty my stomach. I come out after washing my hands and splashing water over my face. "Aunt Mary, I think I need to lie down for a while, my stomach is really upset. Maybe I won't eat tonight."

"I'm sorry Karen. Yes, go ahead and lie down. I'll check on you a bit later. We've had a busy day. Goodness knows these last months have been extremely hard on you. If you aren't up in the morning when I leave and feel like you can eat, you can warm some Quiche."

I feel a little chilled when I pull back the sheets on my bed. I never get sick. I sure hope this is gone by morning. I came here to recuperate, not spend my visit in bed. The sheet feels cool against my arms. I look at the chair beside the dresser. Jess's robe is flung over the back of it. I get out of bed and wrap myself in his smell. I climb back into bed, push my head and shoulders into the feather pillow and breathe in the memories from Jess's robe, memories I never want to forget.

I wake in the morning, but now I feel worse. The gurgle in my stomach makes sounds like a boiling pot of water. This is crazy. Now I feel like I have to throw up. Yep, better get to the bathroom. Does food poisoning feel like this? Don't know and I sure don't like it.

The house is quiet. Aunt Mary's note sits by the coffeepot. "Gone to the library. Be home after eleven. Warm up some food. Make yourself at home. Love, Aunt Mary."

I take a second look at the coffee pot still steaming. I love coffee, yet my stomach screams a big no to me right now. I open a cupboard to see if there are some crackers. My mother always tells me crackers help a sour stomach. Saltines, just what I need. I pull two crackers out of the box and gingerly bite the tip off one. I chew slowly; to make sure the cracker is going to stay down. So far… so good.

I open the refrigerator to get bottled water because the cracker feels like it won't go down my throat. I glance at the clock. It's already ten-thirty. Aunt Mary will be home in an hour. Maybe I should get dressed and wander around the farm. I'll go see Ibn.

Ibn whinnies when he sees me. It sure feels good to be remembered. I hurry my steps. I flop my body on to the rail fence and hang over to wrap my arms around Ibn's neck. "Hi buddy. Shall we take another ride this afternoon? Just soon as my tummy stops wiggling buddy, that's what we'll do." The other six horses in the arena vie for my attention.

Shortly after eleven thirty, Aunt Mary comes home. She carries a paper grocery bag. "Hey Karen. How are you feeling this morning? I stopped at the store to get some Ginger Ale and some antacid just in case you weren't better."

"Thanks, I feel about the same. I can't imagine what's wrong with me. You didn't get sick and we ate the same thing. I've got a strong stomach too. Jess used to say I had an iron stomach because I can eat spicy foods. He never liked spicy foods much." I flinch at the memory.

"Well, I have the stuff just in case. I'll plan a bland lunch and dinner. One step at a time, right Karen?"

The rest of the day my stomach rumbles and clenches. I try to eat a dry turkey sandwich for lunch. It stays down, but the nauseous feeling doesn't go away. For dinner, I eat a small helping of brown rice and a piece of chicken we grill outside while we watch the sun, once again, sneak behind Lone Mountain.

After dinner, we slouch down into the soft leather chocolate-colored couch. I grab one of the squishy pillows and hold it snug against my tummy.

When I was in college I used to watch television when I was supposed to be doing homework. One of these old shows is on tonight. It's about a bunch of college girls. One of them discovers she's pregnant. She's only a freshman and is shocked and worried about what her boyfriend might say.

I squirm a little and push the pillow deeper toward my tummy. It suddenly hits me; smacks me right between the eyes. With all that's been going on, me being in the hospital for so long, Jess' death, all the medication I've been on, I breathe in and quickly sense fear tightening my chest. Dear God, could I be pregnant? Of course, I don't remember the early weeks in the hospital but I know for sure I've not had a menstrual cycle. I just assumed it was because of the trauma to my body, the emotional stress and of course, my age.

Chapter Fifteen

I wake on my fourth day in Arizona extremely troubled. I'm still very nauseous. I didn't sleep because I couldn't quiet the thoughts bouncing in my head. A pounding headache kept me awake. Should I tell someone about my concern? Maybe I should call Mom or maybe I should go home. Slow down Karen, I warn myself.

I smell bacon. Aunt Mary must be up. I get dressed and when I button my jeans this morning I think they feel a little snug. I'm paranoid for sure. But when I tug on the zipper, I fall back on the edge of my bed and I can't hold back the tears starting to trickle down my cheeks and land on the front of my light blue shirt. They leave dark spots across my chest.

I control my tears; rinse my face and head to the kitchen. Aunt Mary looks up from stirring some eggs into a frothy mix. "Hi honey, I thought I'd make some pancakes this morning. They will be easier for you to digest with a bad tummy." She pours the egg mixture into flour and starts to whip again. When I don't answer her, she stops. "Karen, honey, you look awful. Do you feel worse?"

I fall into her arms and bury my head on her shoulder. She holds the whisk with one hand. It drips batter on the floor. I sob. She turns me slightly before she drops the whisk into the sink and pulls me from her so she can wipe my tears with a hand towel she picks up from the counter. "Karen, do you think you might be pregnant?"

Her words sting more than the wasp experience I had in my childhood. "Oh, Aunt Mary, I don't know. What will I do? Jess and I never talked about children. Gosh, my kids are grown. No way could this be possible, could it?" I pull away so abruptly I stumble over a kitchen chair. Aunt Mary catches me and keeps me from doing a face plant right here on the kitchen floor. She sits me in a chair and bends down on her knees in front of me.

"Karen, listen to me. I'm going to call Doctor Anderson. We'll get you in to see her this week. You have had so much stress and pain. If you are indeed pregnant, you need to know so you can start taking special care of yourself and the baby."

"No, no, I can't be pregnant. Not without Jess. I won't be pregnant without Jess." I feel sicker now; my heart hurts and I want to throw something and scream! I bolt out of the chair, shove the back door open and run. I run toward the barns, past the arenas. Ibn squeals at me with a sharp whinny. I run faster. I'm out of breath before I open one of the empty stalls in the barn. I fall to my knees into a thick layer of sawdust shavings. "Why God, is this happening? I hate you. I can't do this. I won't."

I don't know how long I lay in the shavings. The stall door opens a couple of inches. Aunt Mary's head arches around the door. "Come on sweetheart. Let me get you back in the house. It has started to cloud up and there is a forecast of rain. The sky is already looking mean." She tugs on my arm, firmly but gently.

I don't look at her. I feel dead. I want to die. My body hurts all over, I want to cry; but all I can do is get up meekly and follow her. She seems to have to hold me in an upright position. My feet don't feel like they are attached to my legs. We make it back to the house just as a heavy wind starts to blow. I feel cold and it's the middle of April.

Aunt Mary tucks me into my bed. I still have my clothes on but she removes my shoes. Before I close my eyes, she reaches over to the chair by the dresser, picks up Jess's robe and throws it over me. I smell him. His smell soothes me.

***

I don't pay any attention this morning to the time when I glance toward my shuttered window. I'm going to stay here all day. I hear my door creak. Aunt Mary comes in. She carries a tray. "Rise and shine princess. I made you some plain toast with just a tad of homemade jam. I made some hot tea too, with a splash of lemon to help settle your stomach."

I pull the covers over my head and bury my nose in a section of Jess's robe. "Thank you, but I don't think I can handle any food." I pull the corner of the blanket off one eye and look up. Aunt Mary smiles and her brows are pinched together. Tiny lines run across her forehead.

"Please..." Now her lips pucker in a pathetic pout.

I peel the covers from my body and sit up. "You are really just too much." I feel my nose wrinkle and I laugh. "Okay, I will try. Okay?"

"Once you are up and about, you'll need to dress because we have an afternoon appointment with Doctor Anderson. We are going to get to the bottom of this. I'm going to finish cleaning the kitchen. Chop, chop." She slaps her hands together.

The door closes and I prop the tray across my lap. I take a sip of the tea and it does taste good. Here I go, I take a bite of the toast and jam, roll it around in my mouth and swallow, so far, so good. I'm hungry. I eat both pieces of toast. When I dress, I convince myself I've gained ten pounds.

***

The doctor's office is busy. It reminds me of the time I sat and watched, with curiosity, all the patients in the room of my own doctor who diagnosed my cancer. I wonder if any of those people had a bad disease or have died. It's kind of creepy to think these things. I glance around this room. Doctor Anderson is a family doctor. I see several children. Most of them are hacking and sniffling. I notice also, most of them aren't trained to cover their mouths with an arm. Actually, I enjoy watching them when they rub their snotty noses on their moms' sleeves. I feel a bit better this afternoon too, so I guess my mood is naturally better.

"Karen Anderson, Doctor Anderson will see you now." I smile because it feels weird the doctor's name is Anderson too. I felt so blessed to become an Anderson when I said my vows to Jess.

I walk into the exam room area alone. Aunt Mary asked if I wanted her to come in but I feel like this is something I need to do by myself. It seems much too unreal to me without Jess. Please God don't let me be pregnant.

The nurse directs me to a room, hands me one of those white gowns with the blue polka dots all over it. I see the room is already set up where the doctor can do a female exam. My heart skips a few beats. I place my hand over my stomach. It feels a little swollen. How come I haven't noticed this before?

"Hello Karen, I'm Doctor Anderson. Pretty cool we have the same last name huh?" She steps close to me and extends her hand. Her grip is firm and confident. I already like her.

"I understand from my good friend Mary you are having a little stomach trouble. She filled me in on all that you have been through these past months. I am so very sorry for your loss." When I don't answer, she says, "How about we just get right to an exam?"

Dr. Anderson motions for me to scoot up on the exam table. I remember how I hate the thin white paper stretching across the pad. I have always thought how useless the paper is since it rips the minute I wiggle to place my body into a position for the procedure.

I remain silent. I don't know what to say. Will she think I'm evil if I tell her I don't want to be pregnant?

She puts gloves on her hands and turns. "I'll just take a pap smear while I'm at it, this way you won't have to come back later. Just relax Karen, it will be quick."

I roll my eyes. Does she think I've never done this before? Just be done with it already. I nod. She sits on her swivel stool. She is rather young. I like this. She has her long thick hair pulled back into a high ponytail. I used to have long thick hair. I touch the sides of my short curly bob. Jess loved my long hair but ever since the chemo, I've kept it short. He teased me often about my cute bob cut. Oh, how I miss him.

My memory is shattered. "Well, Karen, everything looks good. You are at least two, maybe three months pregnant. I don't see..."

"No." I pull my legs up and push myself into a seated position. "No, I don't want to be pregnant. I'm too old. I don't have a husband. Are you sure?" I feel the shake start in the arches of my feet. Within seconds it travels up my thighs and torso. I feel like I can't breathe. The doctor rushes to my side.

"It's all right Karen." She puts an arm around my shoulders. "Breathe deep through your nose and then let the air out slowly." A nurse comes in. Dr. Anderson nods to her. "Could you please go to the waiting room and ask Mary to come in here? Karen, why don't you lie back for just a minute."

I feel like I'm going to pass out. My head feels clammy and hot. The room spins. "Okay." I gulp between the deep breaths. "I think I'm okay. Just let me lie here a minute."

Aunt Mary comes into the room and stands next to me. She rubs my forehead. The look on her face makes me feel sad. I think I disappoint her. Her eyes look pained, almost squinted shut.

"I'm sorry Aunt Mary."

"Shush, Karen. Don't be silly, honey. You don't need to be sorry about anything. I am right here and will be with you on this journey. I've called your mother and dad because I feel like you need their support. They are going to try to get a plane to Arizona this evening. Please don't be mad at me."

"I'm not mad at you, Aunt Mary; but please don't call my kids. Okay?" I'm a bit aggravated; after all, I'm forty-two years old. It's not like I'm still in high school. Then again, maybe there is reason for concern for a forty-two-year-old to be pregnant! I think Aunt Mary knows what I'm thinking because she shrinks away from my side.

"Of course, Karen, whatever you say."

I feel like such trouble. None of them will understand what I feel. I know Aunt Mary did what she felt is best, but no one is going to understand. I cannot have this baby without Jess. I touch her on her shoulder. "Can we go home? I need to get out of here."

"Yes, of course. I'll go pay the bill and wait for you in the truck."

We leave. Why do my parents think they need to come? The whole thing is ridiculous. I'm not going to have a baby! My kids are old enough to have children for heaven's sake. No Jess, no baby.

Is the avalanche in my way growing larger? Will peace ever settle in my soul?

Chapter Sixteen

The next morning Aunt Mary tells me my parents will arrive between eleven and twelve o'clock. They're going to get a rental car, but should be at the house before one-thirty. Good, this gives me a few hours to saddle Ibn and spend some much-needed time alone to decipher the past twenty-four hours.

Saddled and ready, I give an easy tap to Ibn's side and we head toward the longest trail on the side of Lone Mountain. It's one of my favorites because it winds almost to the top of the mountain where the view is incredible. The rain cleared up late last night, which gives the air a crisp freshness. Ibn's long strides don't even kick up any dust because the rain packed the trail with moisture. A coyote wanders off to my left. He glances at me as if to say hi, and he puts his nose back to the ground, obviously searching for a small creature for breakfast.

I start to talk to Ibn. "What am I going to do Ibn? I can't have a baby." At the sound of my voice, Ibn cocks an ear to one side. I know it sounds silly, but I feel like he understands me. We spent a lot of time together over the years. My uncle always told anyone who would listen that Ibn and I were meant for one another. I pull up on his rein with a touch between my fingers. He stops. We sit on top of the world, here on this mountain.

I scream from deep in my lungs. "Why God? Never. This will not happen. I won't do this without Jess." I clinch my fingers into a fist and wave it to the sky.

When I check my watch, and see it's time for me to head down the mountain to face Mom and Dad, who by this time will be at the ranch, my back bristles a bit. Do they think I'm sixteen and feel they have to rush here because I'm pregnant? I can make my own decisions! I startle Ibn because instead of a gentle nudge, I kick him hard in his side.

He breaks into a trot and once we are off the mountain, I give him a little more leg and he breaks into his long stride cantor, then a gallop. A breeze blows against my cheeks. I brush some of the short curls from my eyes.

I blink tears from my eyes because the thought running through my mind pulls at my heart. I dig my heels deep into Ibn's side and I yell. "Faster Ibn, faster." Ibn's stronger pace exhilarates my soul; the sides of my shirt whip in the air away from my side. I see the rental car in the distance. It's parked next to my aunt's truck. My parent's lean against the rail fence of the first pasture and my aunt rests against her truck. Ibn and I arrive at a full gallop.

"Whoa." Ibn stops. I lean onto Ibn's neck and caress him under his mane.

Aunt Mary takes hold of Ibn's rein. I jump down, fumble with my gloves and face my parents. "Mom, Dad, it's good to see you but I don't know why you came because I will be home in a couple of weeks." I wonder if I sound a tad too casual.

"Same old Karen." My dad pulls on my right ear. "We just thought news of another grandchild was good enough reason to rush out here. Have you told the kids?" He runs his finger down the tip of my nose and gives it a tap. Mom stares at me; her chin seems to quiver. Is she going to cry?

I'm tempted to make a scene, to tell them I'm not going to have this baby. Instead, I say, "Let's all go inside, shall we?"

Aunt Mary speaks up. "Yes, do, all of you. The door is open. I'll take care of Ibn and give the horses their afternoon oats." She pushes me from behind. "Go."

Once we get settled on the couch in the living room, I let the words fly. "Mom, Dad, I'm not going to have this baby. I can't take care of a baby alone. I won't do it without Jess. You have to understand. Oh, and please don't tell the kids."

My mom grabs my dad's arm. I see by the indentation in his sleeve she is freaked out. Dad clears his throat. "Do we have any input into this Karen? Don't you think you might want to talk to Pastor Rodney?" Now, my mom weeps openly and turns her face into my dad's shoulder.

"Right now, Daddy, I need this time here to do some healing. My heart needs healing. I'm aware of how hard this decision might be for you to hear, for anyone who knows me, but this is my body, my life without Jess and my right to control its destiny. I'd appreciate it if we don't speak of any of this again. Thank you." I feel like I just delivered a speech to a jury. I turn to leave the room. "I'm going to pour some lemonade. Do either of you want some?"

I know when I leave the room I have crushed my parents. But, it has to be. I only hope they will return home and let me be the adult I am, in charge of my life. Aunt Mary comes into the kitchen from outside, just as I pour a full class of lemonade.

"Hi, my parents are in the living room. You may need to console them because I just told them I'm not going to have this baby." I love my aunt. She doesn't say a word. She tips her head toward the open door and walks past me.

I wait and sip my drink for at least twenty minutes before I return. There is a hushed feeling in the silence of the room. Mom's eyes are red, her cheeks splotched pink and her hand still digs deep into Dad's arm. My dad moves to stand and lifts my mom's arm bringing her to stand next to him. "We are staying at the old Jones Inn down the street. We will be taking the first flight out tomorrow. We think you are making a mistake, Karen, but we respect you and love you. We hope you will pray about this. We will pray about this. We don't support your decision and pray you will change your mind."

I sit on the couch and feel numb. What am I doing? I've never seen so much pain in my father's eyes. My mom looks downright ill. All I can do is stand and embrace them. I hold them as tight as my arms can muster.

"I know you don't understand. I'm so lost. Please forgive me. Right now, I don't know what I'm going to do or where I want to go. I've had a job offer here in Arizona." I step back, still holding their hands and at last the tears fall. I see Aunt Mary behind my parents dabbing the corners of her eyes. I've hurt them all. "I'm so sorry." I turn and race to my bedroom.

Chapter Seventeen

Just short of a week on the ranch and I have managed to upset my parents, disappoint my aunt and feel so miserable about myself I don't want to get out of bed this morning. Last night I dreamed about abortion. How many days is it supposed to be safe to terminate a pregnancy? I'm sure it's past the so-called safe time. Pray, my dad said. Why, I ask? God didn't do me any favors when He killed Jess. I roll to my side and bury my face in the comfort of Jess's smell.

By the time I get out of bed and look out the window, my aunt is already bent over the veggies in her garden. So many veggies have already sprouted. The rain we had must have given them a real boost. I wash up, nibble on a piece of toast and head to the barn.

"Morning Aunt Mary. How's the garden doing?" I don't even wait for her answer. "I'm going to saddle Ibn and ride over to Mr. Green's. When I get back, I can do any chores you need done or go to the store for you, just let me know."

She raises her head, which is donned with a big floppy red hat. She waves a gloved hand which lets loose of the rich soil she has dug in. She hollers back. "Looking good honey. Have a good ride but be careful. Don't ride too hard, okay?"

I smile because I understand what she really means. She is worried about me being pregnant and riding. Hmm, I never thought about riding as a deterrent to my baby. Did I just say 'my baby'? My stomach tightens.

***

I lift Ibn's hooves one by one to clean them. When I pick up a back one, he turns his neck and nose into the back of my jeans. I can feel him nibble at my backside. A good feeling tickles up my spine. Oh, how I love this kind of life. Maybe I'm meant to live here. I think I will talk to Mr. Green after all.

The stretch to the Green's is long enough to get a decent run out of Ibn. He loves to gallop. I think all horses love the feel of freedom when they can gallop for a long distance. I know I love it. At the same time, I feel a little voice inside me say ride harder. I'm ashamed because I know by riding hard and fast it might be detrimental to this pregnancy.

Right now, I actually want to lose this baby: my body, my right, and my decision. I turn a corner approaching a desert path, gather the reins and give Ibn an extra jab to go even faster. I have to do a little meandering to get around some of the homes since so many have been built in the last few years, but eventually we speed down the tree-lined road to Mr. Green's. I feel breathless. Ibn breathes a bit hard too; after all, he is older. I think he will live as long as his sire, who was twenty-eight.

Just as I pull on the reins to bring Ibn to a halt, Jim comes down one side of a paddock on a tractor. He turns the engine off. "Hey girl, what's your hurry? What brings you to visit?"

"I came to visit with your dad. Hope he's around?"

"I just finished working on a fence. It's almost lunchtime and we get together in the sales center today with Sub sandwiches. Tie Ibn up there by the office and you can hitch a ride with me." His welcome, wide smile is all I need to accept his offer. I get to the side of the tractor and Jim leans over to grab my hand. He pulls me on board with little effort. We try to talk over the loud tractor engine. Jim motions to me by pointing at his ear that he can't hear me. So, we bump and rumble to the sales center. Jim puts out both arms to offer me safe descent. "Everyone will be glad to see you Karen."

Indeed, the whole Green clan greets me with hugs and happy faces. Kent and Phyllis tow Jacob in a red wagon. Mr. Green rushes over to lift me off my feet in one of his bear hugs.

Jim pulls a chair back from the table they have set up and takes his hat off with a gallant sweep. "Your seat, my lady." Everyone laughs.

I feel so at home with these people. Phyllis brings a large plate of Sub sandwiches to the table along with coleslaw, pickles and bags of assorted chips. I didn't know how hungry I really was. My mouth starts to water as I look at my plate and in a few minutes, I devour a half Sub, chips and two, no three pickles.

Jim winks at me. "So, Karen. You love pickles?" The whole gang looks down the table at me. They laugh. I wiggle in my chair. Do they know?

I help clean up and when I get a moment I ask Mr. Green if it's possible for me to talk privately to him. He agrees and invites me to his office. It's a beautiful office, one of those manly looking kinds with the dark leather couch and chairs to match. His desk front is intricately carved with Arabian horse heads. Bronze western pieces grace all of the tables and shelves. What appears to be thousands of ribbons, plaques and medals pepper the walls. He certainly has been a successful showman and breeder.

"Well my dear, what can I do for you?" Mr. Green eases his back in his chair behind his desk. His hands rest folded on his desk. I smile because he still has the habit of rolling his thumbs over each other while his fingers are clasped together.

"I've been thinking about that job offer. I know I've only been here close to a week, but I feel like I belong back in Arizona. I know you are aware of my accident and what I've been through and still you don't ask questions. Thank you."

He nods and smiles. He has the same look of concern my doctor back home had in his eyes, when he told me I had cancer.

"Well," I start. "I'm thinking I want to accept your offer." I watch his shoulders. They seem to sink into the soft leather before he leans forward and rests his chin on top of his folded fingers.

"Welcome to the team Karen." He stands and comes around the desk. His eyes look slightly wet. "Welcome to the Green family. We work hard, Karen, but we are a family. From the grooms who care for the horses, to the trainers and even the team who feeds and cleans stalls, we are family and we are loyal to one another. I can see all of this in you. Welcome."

I'm so taken aback I can't move. I must be in heaven. This is great. I trip over my own feet with excitement when I tand and he pulls me into one of his bear hugs.

He turns me toward the door. "Let's go tell the rest of the family. We have a lot of time to discuss details, bring your stuff to the ranch… you know, all that kind of minor business."

Chapter Eighteen

When I leave the Green Ranch, I leave with a purpose. The ranch hands have watered Ibn and given him a small piece of hay. He feels fresh under my legs. I ride home and before I know it, I have urged Ibn again into a full gallop. I feel good about the decision I've just made. A fresh start; this is what I need. Jess would be proud of me.

Aunt Mary waves at me from the side of the house. I can't wait to share the news with her. My parents and friends will be harder to convince that this is a good decision for me. Debee and Tom will understand and eventually Pastor Rodney, hopefully he may even one day forgive me for all I'm not.

"Did you have a good visit?" My aunt's damp hair bobs in ringlets. This shows me she is fresh out of a shower. Her shirtsleeve is shorter than the one she wore in the garden. I see proof the sun has drawn a red line where the other sleeve ended and pinked her arms to her fingertips. Her smile is something I love. She seems to have it permanently attached to her face. Tonight, I need her smiles.

"Oh, yes Aunt Mary, I have so much to tell you. I'll get Ibn settled and we can talk over dinner. Let me take you to the diner for supper. You've worked so hard in your garden all day. I just need to take a quick shower. How about it? Deal?" I don't wait for an answer before I nudge Ibn forward and head for the barn.

Dinner goes better than I imagine. Aunt Mary looks genuinely thrilled about me staying in Arizona and working for Mr. Green. We talk while we eat our burgers, then we talk all the way home. Once we sit in the living room our chatter continues. I wish I could comfortably sit with my mom and dad like this. I reach to pick up my teacup when I feel a sharp pain across my abdomen. I wince and bend at the waist.

My aunt puts her hand on my knee. "Karen, are you all right? What is it, dear?"

More pain comes in ripple form… one stab right after another. "I don't, don't know. I'm feeling really nauseous too. I think I'm going to be sick. I need to get to the bathroom." I get up so fast my hand hits my teacup and it shatters on the wood floor. I run to the nearest bathroom next to the kitchen.

Aunt Mary runs behind me. I feel like I'm wetting myself. When I get to the bathroom and look down, blood drips from the bottom of my jeans. "What's happening

Aunt Mary?" I barely pull my jeans down, when a stream of blood pours into the commode. I bend at my waist and cover my eyes with my hands.

Aunt Mary puts her hand on my back. "Just breathe Karen. You are going to be all right. I'm going to get you to the emergency room though because it looks like you have miscarried and a doctor will need to make sure you don't need a medical procedure to prevent infection." She gets down on her knees and lifts my chin. "Did you hear me? I'm going to get you a pair of sweat pants from your room to slip on and we'll go."

It takes me a few minutes to understand what my aunt tells me. I've miscarried. I'm not going to have a baby. I still cramp and my legs shake. Am I relieved, sad, or in some sort of shock? Aunt Mary is back in the bathroom with my sweat pants. She helps me clean up and when I glance back, I see the bloody remains of what used to be my baby. Is this my fault? I don't feel any remorse.

"Okay Karen, just hold on to me and I'll get you to the truck."

Gone, my baby is gone. My aunt holds on to me, opens the truck door and gives my behind a slight push up into the seat. She runs around the front of the truck to the driver's seat, jumps in and puts the truck into gear.

At the hospital, the nurses and staff are very helpful and kind. A doctor checks me out physically and declares the miscarriage looks clean and complete. He doesn't think I will need any other procedures other than rest, lots of liquids and emotional support. I don't respond to anything because I feel numb. The only thought my brain releases is, I've purposely ridden Ibn hard because I knew this was a possibility. I rode Ibn hard and actually hoped I'd miscarry. Is God going to punish me?

I climb into the truck by myself and remain silent during the trip back to the ranch. Aunt Mary hums to a country western tune on the radio. She doesn't say a word. I wonder if she is thinking my same thoughts. Will she blame me? I start to feel convicted, but I'm really glad I don't have to worry about a baby. After all, isn't this perfect now? I can move here and start a new job, a new life.

Aunt Mary is out of the truck and opens my door. She reaches her hand out to assist me. I wave her hand away and slip to the ground. She looks at me. Her eyes seem to drip with sympathy. I fall into her embrace and cry, really, the kind of cry where I empty my grief. I cry for Jess, but... I bet she thinks I'm crying about the baby. All the while, she just whispers, "Hush,

hush, little one, you'll get through this trial too. God loves you."

I cringe on her last words. How can God love me? I've just killed my child. I tell God every night in my prayers how angry I am with Him. I even said I hate you God. I leave my aunt and go right to my bedroom. Without undressing, I climb on to my bed and wrap myself up with Jess's robe and cry until I feel the lids of my eyes get heavy from exhaustion. My last thought before giving in to sleep is, what will Aunt Mary do with my baby. Did it even look like a baby?

Chapter Nineteen

A week passes. I spend most of my time resting. It's easy to do around the serenity of the ranch. Spring has definitely arrived. Aunt Mary's garden and all the multitude of flowers and bulbs she plants are all in full bloom of yellow, red and purple. Hummingbirds by the dozens flutter their tiny wings to vie for the sweet water in my aunt's numerous red feeders. I wake up to glorious pink and orange sunrises and bathe in the beauty of equally stunning sunsets at night. This is a haven for rest.

I miss being able to ride Ibn, but my doctor tells me I can start soon. My aunt told the Greens I had some sort of flu, but Mr. Green visits anyway and we make plans to move my things to the little house on his property. Jim told his father he can drive one of the eight passenger ranch vans back to my home in Texas. He will remove most of the seats and there will be plenty of room for my things, especially since the house is furnished and I don't have to haul anything too large.

My mom and dad seem to be excited about my new venture and are supportive.

They say all the normal things when I tell them about my miscarriage, "We're so sorry Karen. It wasn't meant to be. God must have other plans for you." Of course, every word they say convicts me. I'm glad I never told my kids or the Green family, no need to for sure.

Aunt Mary has already been at the cottage I will live in at Mr. Green's. Her artistic hands are making the little house very girly, but at the same time simple. I'm so grateful for our relationship. I see some similarities between my aunt and her sister. Mom is artistic too and our home makes people feel at home and welcome.

***

Moving day is here. Jim pulls the van close to the back door of Aunt Mary's house. I shove a small bag of clothes and essentials for the trip into the van. I look in the back and Jim's German Shepard dog, Trouble lounges on a large crumpled bed. Jim tips his hat in my direction. "Hope you don't mind Karen, but I just have to bring Trouble along. He won't be any bother; besides he can't function without me." His hardy laugh fills my heart with a surprised heated flush.

I nod and give him a thumb's up. I smile on the inside because I remember how

Jess always told me he wanted a German Shepard puppy. Must be a guy thing. We finish loading. I turn to my aunt. Again, her strong eyes bore into mine.

"Be safe Karen. I can't wait till you get back. Jim will take good care of you." She hugs me and gives me one of her notorious pats on my behind. "In you go girl."

She rushes to the driver's side. "Now, you, young man, drive the speed limit and bring her back here safe and sound. I'll look in on the Green gang so don't be worrying about them." As we drive away, she waves one of those funny little hand movements like the beauty queens do when you see them in parades. I start to laugh.

Jim reaches to turn on the radio. "Anything special you'd like to hear, Karen?"

When I shake my head, he flips a station to old classics. Jess and I loved the classics. I sit back in my seat. We ride in silence.

The next thing I realize, we are almost at our halfway point. The lull of the ride must have put me to sleep. I had lain awake all night thinking about the trip. I'm a bit embarrassed. I must have slept through gas stops as well. Talk about feeling foolish! "Oh my gosh Jim, I'm so sorry to be such a poor travel companion. I didn't sleep much last night. Guess I was excited about the trip." I sit up, stretch and offer him a grin.

"It's all right, you must have needed the rest. Think we might stay up the road a bit for the night. There is a motel a couple of hours just off the highway on our right. Okay by you?"

"Yes, sounds great." I fiddle with my hair. I push my hair behind my ears and apply some lip balm. Small talk makes the next few hours feel like mere minutes.

The hotel looks decent when we pull up to the entrance. Jim suggests I stay put ... he says he'll get the rooms and then we'll drive around the motel to a parking spot. Once tucked into our rooms, I pull my cell phone out of my jeans and call Mom and Dad.

"Hey Dad, it's me. We just got to a motel. We'll probably get a quick bite to eat, get some rest and leave early in the morning. We should get to your house by evening."

I hear him sigh. "I'm so glad to hear your voice. Mom and I can't wait to see you. You tell Jim he better take good care of our princess."

"Yes Dad, I will." I smile to myself. He still thinks I'm his baby. We have a few minutes of small talk before I hear Jim's knock on the door. "Got to go, Jim's at the door. Love you."

Jim and I head across the street to an Outback Restaurant. It feels easy to be with Jim even though we were only casual friends when my family lived in Arizona. As he studies the menu, I steal a look at him. He has grown up. Ha, haven't we all? His soft brown hair keeps falling across his forehead. Most of the time, he doesn't try to push it back. Suddenly, he cocks his head sideways and looks at me.

"Something wrong?" he asks just as he flips his head slightly and the hair on his forehead moves back in place.

"No, no. Do you know what you're going to have?" I point a finger at the menu.

"Yeah, probably the six-ounce sirloin." He bends his head again to scan the menu. "And maybe a baked potato. How 'bout you?"

This is when I become aware how blue Jim's eyes are, also how wide his smile is. I think I blush before I answer. "Uh… the same I think. Sounds good." I put the menu down and take a sip of my water. Well, this is awkward, I think.

Our stomachs full, Jim grabs my hand and we race across the street like teenagers. Our conversation seems so easy and genuine at dinner, like a couple of old friends reliving memories of when they were little.

When we get to our rooms, Jim gives me a salute. "Be ready by 6:00 a.m. sharp. I'll be up earlier 'cause I need to feed Trouble and make sure he does his business before we head out. Sleep tight."

Before I fall asleep, my mind wanders. How long will I feel this pain? Will I ever fall in love again? Jess and I used to talk about deep subjects like, what would we do if one of us dies. He always told me he didn't want me to grieve for a long time and to remember he'd be in heaven, in the best place in the world. I never quite understood how he could feel so good about being dead. I told him I never wanted to live without him. He usually ruffled my hair with his knuckles and said, "Because you believe in Jesus, Karen, you will see me again if I die before you. Meanwhile I'd want you to be happy, no matter what."

I fall asleep and dream about heaven and Jess.

Chapter Twenty

My heart squeezes tight for a second when we round the corner into my parents driveway. Dad is in the front yard. He is bent over his prize roses. They are already starting to bud. Dad is a genius when it comes to roses. Every year he wins a prize at our local fair. He seems to hear the van approach because he turns to wave at us.

Jim puts the van in park and I jump out and run toward my dad. He is still strong enough to pick me up and swing me in a circle. "How's my girl? Gosh, it's good to see you." He plants butterfly kisses all over my forehead before he releases me.

"Mom. Come out. Our girl is here."

He walks over to Jim and pulls him into an embrace. "Long time, Jim. You look wonderful. Good to see you."

I hear the front door slam and Mom runs toward me. She pulls me into a tight hug. I see drops of moisture on her lashes.

"Aw, Mom, don't cry. We are here safe and sound. Yes, yes, I love you too."

She hugs me tighter.

Jim walks beside us and wraps his arms around my mom's waist. "Yes, Mrs.

Smith, I drove like an adult and did the speed limit." His grin reaches his ears.

Mom grabs Jim's hand and swings toward him. "Just look at you, Jim. What's it been, about five years? Well, get your things and come on in the house. I've kept supper warm on the stove." We all giggle at the genuine fondness we have for one another, and step into the house.

Before we start to eat, Jim asks if he can say grace. My parents nod and bow their heads. I'm taken aback a little, but shouldn't be surprised by his request since this is normal makeup for the Green family.

I feel uncomfortable when he offers me his hand. He wants us to hold hands. I reach for my mom's hand, and then take his as well. I'm reminded Mom and Dad do go to church occasionally, so I'm sure they don't think anything about this, but right now I'm still not very happy with a God who kills people. I bow my head anyway.

Dinner conversation is all about our agenda to pack my belongings and get me moved to Arizona. Dad has already met with my landlord and made all the arrangements for me to be able to vacate. He has paid my rent in full up to the end of the week, which gives me four days. I'm one lucky girl to have such support from my parents. Since I haven't returned to work, my budget is tight in spite of the life insurance policy Jess left.

We spend the rest of our evening in the living room. We chat about memories of the two families, those times when our family lived in Arizona and later when we visited Aunt Mary.

Dad finally tells us, "Well, it's time for us old people to hit the bed. We've made up a room for you, Jim, down the hall. Of course, Karen's room is just as it was before she went off to college." He rubs his hand across my cheek and plants a kiss on the top of my head.

Mom starts to clear the table. Jim jumps up and holds out his hand. "Mrs. Smith, don't worry about the dishes, I'm a great washer and I'll bet Karen can dry up a storm."

I assure Mom Jim is right. "Thank you, you two. We'll see you in the morning." I wink at Mom and walk toward the kitchen.

Jim has already started the water and added the soap. I grab a towel and stand at attention. "Yep, I stand ready. The dry queen of the west." We both laugh.

Morning peeks through the curtains in my bedroom. I can't remember when I slept so soundly. I smell coffee brewing and hear the clank of dishes. Mom must be up making breakfast. I'd best get in the shower and get out there.

When I reach the kitchen, Dad flips pancakes, coffee is poured and Jim and Mom sit at the table. They talk in a whisper.

"What's so secretive?" I grab a cup of coffee and tip the cup in their direction.

Mom pushes her chair back, reaches up and pulls my face down to hers where she kisses my cheek. "No secrets honey, we were talking about our schedule today, you know, where to start first."

I sit down. "I'm all for going to the apartment right after breakfast to get started."

Mom hesitates. "Karen, you know, don't you, it might still be hard for you."

I love my mom for her tenderness. "Yes, Mom, I do but at the same time I also know it's something only I can do, you know, sort through things we need to pack. Do you know if Debee has been at the apartment?"

"Yes, she called a week ago to let me know she had been there."

"Then we're good Mom. It will be okay."

On the way to the apartment, I tell Jim about the neighborhood and point out some of the highlights of our community. He listens and nods. I feel like I'm the only one talking. I guess I am. I'm kind of rambling. There I go. I'm pulling at the ends of my hair again. Thought that old habit was long gone. Guess not.

Jim and I reach the apartment first. It looks just the same. Oh for heaven's sake Karen, it hasn't been that long. I unlock the door, when I suddenly feel my legs start to shake and my heart races. Jim seems to understand what's happening, so he steps in front of me and pushes the door inward. He flips on a light switch because the shutters are all closed, and walks in ahead of me.

Chapter Twenty-One

I'm surprised I feel so unraveled. I've only been gone a few weeks, yet the rooms of my apartment feel foreign. I note right away Jess's personal items I left in the living room are gone. Debee appears to have followed my directions. I walk to our bedroom. When I open our closet door, my knees buckle when I see my clothes hanging neatly on one side of the closet and an empty space occupying the other half. I guess I didn't realize the empty space might make my stomach churn. I clutch my arms around my waist and fall to the floor. I cry out, "No, God no," and collapse with sobs. My entire chest starts to burn.

"Karen, are you alright?" Jim is at my side with his hand on my shoulder. "What can I do? Here, take my hand. Let me get you to the side of your bed."

I look up at Jim. The concern and pain I see in his eyes tells me he really does understand and wants to help. I feel his compassion. I take hold of his hand. He gently guides me to sit on the edge of my bed.

"I'm so sorry Jim, I had no idea it would be so hard to come back here and find all of Jess's things gone. I told my girlfriend to remove his things but I, I never thought…" Tears consume me again. I lie across the bed and cry with so much pain, it feels like I'm never going to be able to stop.

"Karen, I know our situations aren't exactly the same but I do understand a great deal of what you are going through. I remember when my mother passed; I thought I'd die. Then when my girlfriend passed away last year, I felt like I'd never get over the loss. I can only tell you, time does help heal. I also have faith to know my mom and Stacy are in heaven where they live forever and someday I'll see them again."

As Jim speaks, his voice has such a soothing effect that I'm able to sit up, rub the back of my hand across my wet nose and compose myself. "Thank you Jim, for trying to make me feel better. I wish I could feel what you just said, but right now I'm not very pleased with God. Jess was too young. It's just not right."

Jim's eyes squint like he is in pain. "It's normal for you to be angry with God, Karen." He moves off the bed and stands. He reaches a hand toward his forehead to brush back that stubborn lock of hair. "It will get better. I think this move will be helpful too. I'll just go into the kitchen and when you feel better, maybe we can start to pack your things." He gives me a quick hug.

Yes, I tell myself, get a grip Karen. I move off the bed slowly and look once again at the open closet door. He's gone Karen. It's just you, kiddo. I walk to the closet and begin to take handfuls of my clothing out and lay them on the bed.

I pull another bundle of clothes from the closet, when I hear my mom and dad's voices. I'm sure Jim is giving them an update on my behavior. I turn to see Mom in the bedroom doorway.

"Hey sweetie, I'll start on the drawers. I assume you want to take all of your personal things?" She steps past me and starts to unfold and tape several boxes she holds under her arm.

"Thanks Mom." I love her even more because she isn't making an issue about me being so sad. Maybe my parents are finally able to understand my craziness.

"You're welcome. Your daddy is in the kitchen. He and Jess are going to pack the kitchen up. It might be a disaster when you go to unpack." She lets out a hardy laugh and I do too.

Dad comes to the bedroom door. "Hey pumpkin, since your new place is furnished, I asked my fixit guy if he could store your furniture for a while until I can get our garage rearranged. He will come by Friday and we can get it out of here and do the cleaning. I had Jim put the rocker in the van, 'cause I figured you'd want that piece to go. Am I right?"

A lump forms in my chest. Yes, the rocker; the one that belonged to Jess's grandmother. "Yes, Daddy. That's just perfect. Thank you."

We finish packing before the sun starts to hide behind the tall buildings. My family is amazing. The guys stacked all the boxes in the van, and left just enough room for Trouble. Mom not only packed and arranged all my clothes; she managed to clean as she went along. Bathrooms sparkled, as did the kitchen floor and even the windows. Dad's fixit guy won't have much to do when he gets the rest of the furniture.

"Well done, family." I put my hands on my hips and tip my head. "I can't believe how much we accomplished. Thank you so much."

"My pleasure." Jim bends forward and makes a sweeping bow with his arms.

Mom gives me a hug and Dad gives me his usual pat on the behind before he whistles and says. "I'm hungry. Who's hungry?"

In unison, we yell, "Me!"

Chapter Twenty-Two

Goodbyes are extremely hard. My parents try to keep a stiff upper lip. Mom lets a few tears pool in the corners of her eyes but quickly brushes them with the back of her hand. I'm sure she doesn't want to get me started. Dad wrinkles his nose and gives me a wink before he picks me up in one of his strong hugs.

Here I come Arizona. I feel confident as we pull away. We'll stay in the same hotel on the way back, only this time I intend to be cordial and stay in conversation with Jim. Maybe I'll offer to drive some as well.

"Looks like the weather will be good, Jim. I checked the app on my phone. I always get nervous this time of the year, you know tornadoes in good 'ole Texas!" I sit back in my seat, adjust my seat belt and gaze out the window.

"Yes, I checked my phone too. What would we do without the technology we have today?" Jim laughs, pushes back that lock of hair and reaches for the radio. "How about a little music?"

Stevie Wonder starts to sing, "I Just Called To Say I Love You." I feel myself getting into the music. I catch Jim out of the corner of my eye and he is keeping time with the ballad by tapping his fingers on the edge of the steering wheel.

"Don't you just love Stevie Wonder?" I tilt my head sideways and raise my eyebrows.

"Actually, I do. I think I have every CD he has ever made. I even have some old cassettes. This song has such a simple lyric, just about loving someone. I place it at the top of songs I could listen to over and over. You?"

"I didn't always love everything he did, but for sure, this song is one of my favorites."

Our conversation is steady. I'm kind of surprised how much Jim and I have in common. We like a lot of the same music. Of course, he loves horses too. How could he not, since he helps run his father's breeding facility? He also loves a good glass of wine and the outdoors, hiking and nature in general. I'm a sucker for all of these things.

The first leg of our trip comes to an end soon. I look forward to getting a good night sleep before we arrive back at the ranch. I look in the side mirror of the van. I'm awed by another sunset forming and framing itself behind us. Arizona sunsets are unbelievable, so I'm a little surprised this Texas one seems to beckon me to stay. "Wow, look at the sky behind us Jim."

"Beautiful, isn't it? God's creations humble me often." Jim's chin comes up slightly and he peeks at the rearview mirror.

There he goes again. I feel a little twinge of guilt. God...why does he always have to bring God into every conversation? I lean back into my seat and remain silent for a short time. Quit it Karen. After all, I did say I would keep Jim company on the way to Arizona.

Our conversation takes many directions. We talk about our families, our college years, close friends and a lot about the ranch. Jim shares he and Kent are taking on more and more responsibility at the ranch because their father can't do quite as much as he used to. I tell him how thankful I am for this job opportunity and how I'm going to do everything I can to help the ranch run smoothly. The sun sets behind us. I realize we are almost at the hotel for our night's stay.

"All right, here we are. I'll go get our room keys. Same routine, clean up, meet for dinner and off in the morning early?"

I smile. "Sounds good."

My alarm goes off at 4:30 a.m. I actually slept soundly once again. I'm really excited about getting back to the ranch. I dress, pack my night bag and make my way to the breakfast bar in the motel. Jim is already scanning the newspaper while holding a cup of coffee. He looks up.

"Morning. Hope you slept well. Have a seat. I'll get you a cup of coffee."

"Great, I will and thanks." Dang. He is so polite. Jess was like this too.

After a few words and some breakfast, we are off again. Arizona here we come. The scenery starts to look familiar. I begin to feel flutters in my stomach. I'm ready for a new beginning.

Chapter Twenty-Three

We've come the northern route on highway 40, now headed down I-17, which used to be called Black Canyon Highway. We turn onto the Carefree Highway east toward Scottsdale. By the time we reach Cave Creek, I can see Black Mountain and a little bit of Lone Mountain in the distance... almost to the ranch.

"Hey Jim, do you think we can stop by my Aunt Mary's before we get to the ranch? I'd just like to let her know we're here and give her a hug."

"You betcha. I need the outhouse anyway." Jim screws up his face like a little boy and pushes his lips forward.

I laugh. I'm really comfortable with Jim. I start to thank God for this blessing but I catch myself. Nope, not going to go there.

It's not even been a whole week since we left and I can't believe how many flowers are in bloom. Even Aunt Mary's garden looks twice its size. When the van pulls into the drive and through the familiar gate, I see Ibn run around in circles in the arena. Could he possibly know it's me?

Aunt Mary must have been in the kitchen to see the monitor when the gate opened to know we arrived. She runs out, dishtowel waving in her hand. Jim puts the van in park and she already has her hand on the door handle.

"Welcome home you two. Can you come in for a few minutes? I just pulled banana bread out of the oven and I have hot water boiling for tea. Was making it for myself but I've got plenty."

I wrap her in a big hug. "Yes, yes, sounds great. Besides, Jim has to use the little boys room." I look over at Jim and I swear I've caused him to blush.

The banana bread is yummy and the hot tea hits the spot. Most of all, just sitting here with Aunt Mary soothes me. She and Mom are a lot alike, but Aunt Mary seems more at peace… about everything. I feel like our relationship will grow strong while I'm here in Arizona. I like the feeling.

We visit and eat for about an hour, when Jim says. "Well girl, I think we best get to the ranch so we can unpack before it gets too dark. Besides, my dad and the rest of the gang are biting at the bit to see us." He stands and puts a hand out to pull my chair back.

"You're right Jim." I push my chair back, wink at my aunt and give her another hug. "Thanks for the banana bread and tea.

It's just what I needed to fuel myself to unpack. I'm so excited we'll be able to spend lots of time together now I'm here."

We say our farewells. Jim whistles for Trouble, who is running loose in the yard. Trouble runs toward us, tongue hanging from the side of his mouth, ears perked, and he leaps in the van on Jim's command. He has been such a good dog the entire trip. Sometimes I forgot he was with us.

I start bouncing in my seat when we get to the long tree-lined lane to the Green ranch. I feel like little butterflies attack my insides. In just a week the trees have really leafed out. The mares' and babies' winter coats are gone. Most likely the grooms have been busy with curry brushes. The stallions walk in circles on the horse walkers. I can see the grooms have worked hard to bring their coats to a glimmering shine, plus most of them have been kept in barns through the winter under heavy blankets.

Jim whistles along with a song on the radio and I can tell he is happy to be home. I listen more intently. Once again, Stevie Wonder sings, "I Just Called To Say I Love You." All of a sudden Jim belts the words out loud. I shake my head. I have no idea what possesses me but I start to sing out loud with him. Just as we turn the corner by the office, I see Mr. Green race down the dirt road in his golf cart. The red, white and blue fringe blows in the breeze.

"Hey y'all," Mr. Green shouts, when Jim slows the truck and rolls down the window. "I've already opened up the cottage, so you can drive on over there. Kent and some of the ranch hands are waiting to help unload. I'll give you a hug when we get there." He turns the golf cart on two wheels and waves us on.

Jim laughs. "That's my pops. He's always one step ahead of us all." He turns the wheel of the van to the right and off we go. Now I'm laughing.

We all pile out. Trouble runs ahead. He barks and jumps on everyone he hasn't seen in a few days. Kent and the ranch hands wave hellos to us and ruffle Trouble's coat behind his ears.

It's not like I had all that much to unload, but we unload in a little over an hour.

We joke about who has the most muscle and of course the men had to make a big issue about how most of what I brought was lots of clothes. One of the sacks falls open and a ranch hand prances around with one of my lace nightgowns on his head.

My stomach hurts from laughing. Finally, I step forward and say. "Okay, enough already. Thank you one and all for your help. I'm truly so grateful. Can I buy pizza for us all? None of us should have to cook after all of this. What do you say?"

It sounds like twenty people instead of five when they all holler, "Yeah, let's eat."

Chapter Twenty-Four

I order six large pizzas and we eat like we haven't eaten in months. I feel so loved and accepted in this family. I can truly see the truth of Mr. Green's statement that they are all one big family, how they are loyal to one another. I hug each one before taking one of the golf carts back to my new residence. I'm genuinely exhausted from the past few days' activities. I shower, change into my jammies, wrap Jess's robe around me and collapse into bed.

My alarm squeals at 5:30 a.m. I decide to get up early so I can walk through the barns before going to the office. I want to say hello to all the help who have to start their days early like this every morning. I want to get to know them, the horses and all it takes to keep Mr. Green's ranch going.

Gosh, it feels good to pull my boots on. How many people get to enjoy a job so much? All my life I dreamed of owning my own horse and here I am living on a ranch, which houses over two hundred of them. While I was in Texas my Aunt Mary had asked Mr. Green if she could bring Ibn over to the ranch, so I could ride him more often. I couldn't believe it when Mr. Green told me they put Ibn in one of the stalls just outside my house. I'm living a dream.

Even at the end of April it feels a little cooler than I expect. As I walk to the main barns, I rub my arms to bring some warmth to them. Once I'm inside the brood mare barn, I take a deep breath and relish the smells of fresh shavings and manure. Remember, I'm weird like this. The lights in the ceiling blaze and the stall cleaners are busy mucking. I stop at the first stall.

"Good morning, just thought I'd start my day by saying hello." I put my hand through the stall grate.

I see real surprise on a young man's face. I think he might be blushing a bit. He takes his glove off one hand and reaches through the bar to take mine in his.

"Morning, good to see you. My name is Josh. Guess you are the new marketing person? Welcome." He backs away and nods. I think he just dismissed me.

"Yes, yes I am. I hope we see each other again. Thanks for your hard work." I move away and wave at him. I feel more confident as I pass through the rest of the barns and continue to greet as many as I can before I need to be in the office. I feel good about my decision to have done this. I'm wearing a big smile when I walk through the office door.

The first person to greet me is Mr. Green's private secretary, Lois. She is a tiny woman about sixty, maybe a tad older. When I first met her years ago, I remember it was the buzz around the ranch that she drove a bright yellow mustang corvette. Rumor had it the police department in Scottsdale knew her personally. Her nickname was "speedo." I want to give her a big hug when she comes toward me.

"Lois, oh my goodness, it's been so long. You look wonderful." I embrace her and I can feel by her squeeze she is equally glad to see me. When I push away from her, we both have a few tears in our eyes.

"Oh Karen, I am so sorry to hear about your husband. I have so many fond memories of you and your family. We are so happy to have you here." She takes my hands in hers. "Come, come, let me show you to your office. I'm going to be the one to train you. It will be such a pleasure and I know you will catch on so fast. Come on."

The rest of the afternoon, Lois and I are engulfed in files of pedigrees, brochures, client lists and photos of the Arabians on the sales list. I feel more or less overwhelmed to say the least, but find the information fascinating and exciting.

Mr. Green comes and goes all day. He often pops into my office with a, "How's it going?" Then, "Well, I'll leave you girls alone.

Looks like Lois has it handled." He always leaves with the wink of an eye and nod. I'm going to love this job!

One bit of information Lois tells me is the rule Mr. Green has about the phones, especially his private one. She looks at me with her chin pointed down and her eyes peeking over the top of her glasses. "Mr. Green insists the phones never ring more than twice before someone answers them. That includes his private line. Now, I'm usually the only one to answer his line so you probably will never have to answer it, but I want you to know this is the only thing he gets cranky about. Other than this, I don't ever see him react poorly to anything." She puts her hand close to my face and taps the end of my nose.

She leaves me alone to study pedigrees and get used to my surroundings. I sit back in my swivel chair and look all around the room. The walls above my desk are covered with ribbons and plaques, just like Mr. Green's office. The only other person in the office is Phillip, the accountant, who is tucked in the very back of the building. He needs quiet, Lois explained.

Lois presented me with a beautiful Kodak camera and told me I would be responsible for taking all the photos of the sale horses. I took photography classes in college because I always thought one day I might do it professionally. I love taking pictures. This is another dream come true.

Starting in the fall, I will be doing the commentary for all the previews of the horses we will present every Saturday throughout the buyers' season. I've never been afraid of public speaking. Gosh, who knows where all this will lead?

Chapter Twenty-Five

As Marketing Director, I research pedigrees. I contact clients from all over the world. I sell horses through private showings and sales auctions. With direction from Lois I get to arrange luncheons for visiting dignitaries. I set up photography sessions for the sale horses. For potential clients, I formulate flyers and sales brochures. Then, there are daily tasks like typing, filing and answering phones keeping me busy.

This morning, Lois leaves the building briefly. She always answers Mr. Green's telephone line but in her absence, when the private line rings more than two times, I nervously answer it. I remember the strict rule; a telephone should never ring more than twice before it's answered.

I pick up the receiver. "Green's Arabian Horse Ranch. This is Karen. May I help you?"

The woman on the other end curtly announces. "White House calling."

I feel my eyebrows knit together and I mockingly say, "Yeah, right. Like I'm Elizabeth Taylor." I hang the phone on the cradle.

Lois walks back into the office. When she passes by my desk, I casually say, "By the way, some fool just called on Mr. Green's private line pretending to be the White House."

I watch her face turn chalk white. "Karen, that WAS the White House calling." How could I know Mr. Green and the President of the United States are long-time friends? Talk about feeling stupid. Lois laughs out loud, pats me on the shoulder and proceeds to her desk to return the call for Mr. Green. This is my first day. I can only imagine how many things I need to learn before I feel really confident.

All of a sudden I hear the intercom blare, "All hands on deck! Stall number thirty- four. Eyeball lost in shavings." My hand flies to my forehead. What? Did I just hear that right? Then again, "Stall Thirty-four, now!"

Lois runs toward my desk. "Go, go. Stall thirty-four." She almost pushes me out the door. "All staff has to go, including the office. Molly has lost her eye."

I head out the door; glad I get to wear boots and not heels, as I start to run toward a barn. I'm confused. Who is Molly? How has she lost her eye? By the time I get outside, five workers are running ahead of me, so I follow close behind. Once I get to stall thirty-four, I see one of the handlers who halters a sweet looking chestnut filly with a nearly white mane and tail. Three more workers, the head trainer and two stall cleaners are in the filly's stall on their hands and knees.

Molly is a beautiful little filly and she lost her eye during a severe monsoon storm when she hit a pole. Mr. Green hired an ophthalmologist to fit her with a glass eye. I listen to the story and I feel myself tear up. Yep, cry baby me. I can hardly believe someone would do something so great for anyone, much less a horse. I'm sure proud to work for such a man.

I make my way into the stall and fall to my knees in the shavings alongside the trainer. He shows me a broad smile. "Want to take that section over there? If you just sift through with your hands a section at a time, you'll be able to feel a hard round ball. "Good luck." Again, he shows me a big smile and chuckles.

I pull my hands through the shavings very slowly. I can't believe my luck. "I think I have it." I pull my right hand through the soft sweet smelling shavings and hold the eye up victoriously for all to see. "Yes, here it is." Everyone starts to applaud.

Then almost in unison they yell, "Beginners luck!" I feel pats on my back. Some are high-fiving and everyone is laughing, glad the ordeal is over.

Mr. Green walks up. "Way to go, Karen. Not bad for the first time no less. Looks like you fit right in. I guess Lois forgot to tell you about Molly? She is one of my Bask daughter's fillies. We gave her to a little girl whose family has a small ranch but can't afford to board her. She volunteers here at the ranch. She has quite an aptitude for riding, plus she wants to show the horse. Next time she's here, I'll introduce you to her."

I'm so touched by his generosity, I want to jump into his arms. I know I can't because he is now my boss, even though he has been my friend for some time. There is so much I don't know about this man, but I know he continues to amaze me.

He waves a hand at everybody and says, "Okay, everyone, back to work. Eyeball found. Thanks to all."

After work, I get back to my house, warm up a can of tomato soup and fix myself a grilled cheese sandwich. What a great day. I get ready for bed and for the first time since I got out of the hospital, I leave Jess's robe hanging on the peg by my bathroom.

I take off my boots and say aloud, "No pebbles in today. Life is good."

Chapter Twenty-Six

I sit here in my small L-shaped kitchen. I'm not getting up as early as I did two weeks ago, when I first started my job but I still get up early enough to see the sunrise come over the mountains. I love that the sunrises and sunsets come over mountaintops here in Arizona. There is always color to awe over. Sometimes the pinks and reds take over and the sky looks like it's on fire. It feels good to have my strength back too.

I'm so busy learning the ropes for my job; I've not had time for much else. Mom and Dad call every other day. The kids, on their own journeys in life call less. Aunt Mary and I get together at least once a week. She lifts my spirits each time because she is so darn positive... and that smile... always on her face. Debee calls too. She sends pictures from her cell phone of her belly. Every time I see the image she sends, I feel convicted all over again. This is the only thought I have a hard time burying. I think less of Jess and last night I folded his robe and put it in a plastic bag and shoved it under my bed.

The Green family has been wonderful. Phyllis and I get along great but again, when I'm around her little boy, Jacob, I get a sick feeling in my stomach. Sometimes I just want to tell God, all right already, I'm sorry. I think by now it should all be forgotten. This is the main reason I don't go to church with the Green family, or my Aunt Mary for that matter, when they ask me almost every week. I just don't 'feel' God or maybe I don't want to. I can't shake the anger I feel... of how a loving God could be so awful to take someone so young. Yeah, I know, lots of people lose tiny children; people die in accidents and on and on. Maybe there is no God. Maybe we are all a part of an energy source like some believe. This is what Jess's parents believe. They didn't even come to our wedding because they wouldn't walk into a church. When he first told me, I nearly fell on the floor. My parents told me his parents didn't even have a service for Jess. I cried. I tried to call them many times after I came home from the hospital but the last time I tried, the number had been disconnected.

Why are all these thoughts racing through my head this morning? Do I just exist? I've lately thought I should see what a Bible feels like in my hands again. I'm not even sure where or if I packed it. I know Jess would not be happy with me but after all, he's not here anymore. It's easy to rationalize all of this when the pain of his death eats at me almost every day. I'm sure God wouldn't forgive me anyway after such a horrible sin. And, if there is a heaven, even Jess must not want anything to do with me.

Quit it Karen, all you do is feel sorry for yourself. What can I be grateful for? I push my shoulders back and stand to look out the window. The barn lights dance in the morning sun. "Aha." I shout. I'm grateful Ibn is so near. I try to ride him every evening now because it doesn't get dark so early. Poor guy, I bet he gets sick of me pouring my heart out to him. Maybe it's good he can't answer me or give me advice. I might not want to hear it. Yep, I'm grateful for this.

Jim is very attentive too. I wonder if he has a crush on me. I hope not, because I'm not ready for a relationship. I'm sure he must know that. He is fun though, and he does make me laugh. I'm grateful for the laughter. Am I just trying to convince myself life is just wonderful? I'm not really sure.

***

Today is a Saturday and I've taken the day off so I can go into town to buy a few things I need. By the time I finish work during the week, it's already close to six; I come home, try to ride Ibn, then fall into bed early after a small bite to eat. I don't have a girlfriend here yet who I can call to accompany me on shopping jaunts. Kent's wife is so busy with her little boy. Maybe I'll meet someone at the Gala dinner Mr. Green is holding next week for Arabian breeders. I best get dressed before the day gets away from me. Maybe I'll even buy a fancy dress.

When I leave the ranch, I'm surprised how much traffic I encounter. Scottsdale has sure grown since I was here last. There is now a grocery store as far out as Pinnacle Peak road. The "West's Most Western Town" is growing up. I stop near Shea Boulevard because I see a Starbucks. I'm dying for a strong cup of coffee. I order my coffee and a lemon bar, one of my favorite goodies. I find a seat by a window.

While casually drinking my coffee, I feel a tap on my shoulder.

"Oh my gosh, aren't you Karen Scott?" A well-dressed woman peers over the top of her glasses.

"Uh, yes, yes I am, but I'm Karen Anderson now." I turn to face her. Something looks very familiar about her. "Do I know you?"

She pulls a chair from another small table, sits down and faces me. "It's me, Sylvia."

I'm floored. I suddenly recognize her. "Sylvia, my goodness, how long has it been?

You look amazing." I feel a little inferior since I'm sitting here in my jeans and boots and she is "dressed to the nines".

She reaches across the table and places her hand on mine. "College, I think. I moved to Arizona to finish my studies at ASU. What are you doing here? I take it you are married?" She points to the rings still on my hand.

I feel a blush creep up my neck. "Actually, I'm widowed, happened during a second marriage for me. My husband was killed in a car accident. I've taken a job out here, you know, kind of a new beginning."

"I'm so sorry Karen." She drops her eyes and fiddles with her shirt collar.

I can tell she's uncomfortable. I twist a little in my chair. "Thank you. Each day gets a little easier, Sylvia. What are you doing in Scottsdale?"

"Well, maybe you remember how I always loved fashion? I opened my own modeling agency after I graduated college. My clients range from kids to people eighty and up. Have you ever considered television or radio work?"

I had just taken a sip of my now cool coffee, and almost spit it at her. "Surely you jest!" I wipe at the coffee dribbling from my chin. "Either you have poor vision or you are senile already." I laugh, but then see that she isn't laughing with me.

"Karen, you need to be kinder to yourself. You are a beautiful woman. You have great facial features, almost a chiseled profile with such a cute button nose poking out.

I remember how great you were in speech class. Never afraid, no matter how many people we faced. Do you remember the assembly presentation? You could be great in television commercials and I can see you doing still photos as well. You know, for magazines and such. Most of my clients are looking for a mature look. Let the tall skinny girls do the runway stuff."

Sylvia paused just long enough for me to take in the fact she is serious.

"I'm sorry." I laugh. "But I don't see myself in any of those roles. I'm actually thrilled with my new job! I'm working in the horse business, wearing boots and jeans."

Sylvia laughs. She pushes her glasses firmly onto the bridge of her nose and looks through them. Her eyes kindle kindness. "I'm going to give you my card. I am very serious. It can be a great way to make some extra money and who knows where it might lead. I would love to stay and visit but I am already five minutes behind for an appointment." She stands and hugs me. Before she leaves, she waves. "Please think about it. And Karen, I really am sorry for your loss. Call me."

Chapter Twenty-Seven

After shopping, I seem to walk with a triumphant gait. I don't know if Sylvia's pep talk gave me some confidence, but I bought a nice dress and some heels after our encounter. I catch my reflection in a store window. I push my growing soft curls from my forehead, turn my head sideways and try to see what she saw. I smile at myself. Not bad, not bad at all.

When I pull under my carport at the ranch I see Jim walking down the path from my front door toward me.

"Hey Karen, I just knocked on your door." He glanced at the pile of packages I hold. "Looks like your day was successful. Can I help you with those?" Before I can answer, Jim reaches for several of the packages.

"Thanks Jim and yes, probably too successful, if you know what I mean, on my salary anyway." We laugh at my comment.

I fish my key from my purse and open the front door. "Just lay them on the kitchen table Jim. Do you have time for a cup of coffee or tea?"

"I do, but I came over because I thought you might want to go to Wiley Wranglers with me tonight. They are showcasing a great western band and the food and drinks are great. You do dance, don't you?"

I wonder if Jim sees the shock on my face. I turn my back to him and reach for the teakettle on the stove. "Gosh Jim, I don't know. I'm a little beat…"

"Aw, come on Karen, it'll be good for you. We don't have to stay long. Maybe have a burger and watch people and listen to the music… that is unless you want to try kicking up your heels for a dance or two. Please." He puckers his lips out to the tip of his nose and puts his hands together as if praying. He looks like a little boy asking to use the car.

"Oh, all right. How about seven o'clock?"

"Perfect." He is already at the front door, his hand on the knob. He tips his hat and is gone. Guess he didn't want a cup of tea.

I sit in the kitchen. How much more shock can I encounter today?

I decide the new dress I just bought will fit the bill for my outing with Jim. I think I'll wear my boots, though, because the blue dress has a full short skirt. I shine my old boots and realize the tiny flowers tooled

in the tops are tiny blue daisies. I will match.
I giggle like a schoolgirl.

***

Jim comes to the door. He hands me a
bundle of daisies he has just picked from
alongside the path to the cottage. The stems
are still dripping from the sprinkler shower
earlier. I'm truly pleased. "Wow, these must
have cost you a fortune." I tease.

"Yes, not easy for a rancher who works
for his cheap father."

I resist an urge to snicker at his
comment. At the end of the walk, I drop the
stem end of the flowers into a bucket I keep
full for watering. "I'll find a vase for them
later. Thanks Jim."

I've said this before. Conversation is
easy with Jim. He seems genuinely
interested in my day. When I tell him about
meeting Sylvia and all she had to say, he tips
his western hat back off his forehead. "You
know, that Sylvia is right, don't you? You
really are pretty and it might be fun to do
something like this part time."

He flips the radio on and once again I
hear, "I Just Called To Say I Love You." Jim
reaches to turn the volume up, and laughs.
He starts to sing along with the radio.

Wiley Wranglers is packed with people. Must be a favorite band with a lot of the crowd. We are able to get a table for two toward the back of the room. I'm kind of glad we aren't in front. The crowd is mostly younger people but there is a sprinkling of people our age and the noise is deafening.

I suddenly think, is this a date? Didn't even dawn on me until just now. I haven't thought about Jess all day. Jess loved country music. We seldom went dancing, but he could really swing with the best of the country dancers. I must look like I'm daydreaming because Jim pokes my arm.

"You okay?" He puts his hand on my shoulder.

"Oh yes, sorry, I was thinking about how Jess and I used to do this often. Did you know he played in a band? They were almost ready to record some of their own work just before he died." I surprise myself that I can talk about this without crying.

"Wow, Karen, that's great. I wish I had known him. Sounds like a great guy."

A waitress interrupts us. "Can I take your drink orders? Margaritas are two bucks until eight, and the special tonight is tacos for a buck a piece."

We order and the night goes smooth. We don't dance but I feel like I am talking to a brother, a best friend. I feel like I can say anything to Jim. He shares his dreams and life with Stacy before she became ill. They were together for two years. He talks about his relationship with God and how it was the only thing sustaining him during his trial. I listen. I mention again how angry I feel and wish I could feel the way he does.

On the drive home, Jim suggests maybe I might attend a growth group of people our age he meets with on Thursday nights. He says it could be an opportunity to meet some other single gals. I assure him I will think about it.

He walks me to the door, tips his hat like the gentleman he is and thanks me for the evening. "Maybe we can do this again sometime. I'm going to church at eleven tomorrow. Text me if you want to come along. The music is contemporary. I'd love to introduce you to our pastor." He doesn't wait for my reply, but turns on his heels and gets into his truck.

Chapter Twenty-Eight

Sunday morning and I'm up early. I didn't sleep very well last night. I can't say why, but I kept waking every hour. Once I rolled out of bed and went to look for Jess's robe before I remembered I had wrapped it and stored it under the bed. This morning I'm going to get dressed and go to the nine o'clock service at Jim's church. I know his family almost always attends the eleven o'clock service. I will sit in back and go unnoticed.

I drum the tips of my fingers on the kitchen table and try to remember where I might have packed my Bible, actually Jess's Bible. I remember. After I sprang the hospital prison and went back to our apartment, I put it in Jess's music chest. Selling his instruments wasn't as painful as letting go of the many songs he wrote during our time together, so I kept the chest. I get up and run to my closet.

I remember now. Dad put it in the van alongside the rocker. He didn't even ask me. I faintly remember noticing it when we unpacked here at the ranch. I look at it now, and I don't know if I can open it.

Here goes. Ah, yes, there it is. Jess loved his Bible. His Bible is well worn and the margins inside are marked with stars and his thoughts on various sections of scripture. I see an asterisk penned in bright red. A few lines are boldly underlined "But those who hope in the Lord will renew their strength. They will soar on wings like eagles: they will run and not grow weary, they will walk and not be faint." (Isaiah 40:31)

A tear falls from my eyes onto the page. I quickly wipe it with my hand. How can I hope in the Lord? I want to soar. I am weary. Will going back to church take away all my pain, my grief? I close the Bible, lay my head on top of it and plead. "Oh dear God, please help me. How can anything good come from all of this?"

I check the clock on my dresser. If I splash my face with water and put on a little mascara, I can get dressed and be at the church in time for the service. I'll just sit in the back anyway, so I can leave before the service ends. This way I can avoid any of the Green family if they are there.

I'm so grateful Mr. Green gave me the little blue Nissan truck. When I asked Dad to sell my car after the accident, I didn't think I'd ever drive again. Debee and Bill bought it. It is perfect for them now that the baby is coming, because it is bigger than

Debee's old Volkswagen. I feel a smile cross my face.

I pull out of my carport and I'm glad to see the Green family cars are all parked in their places. Good. Looks like none of them are going to the early service. The church is only a few miles from the ranch. The morning is perfect. Not a cloud in the sky; blue, blue everywhere. The parking lot is full. Only a few people rush toward the doors of the church. I'm able to make my way in and sit in the last row of seats.

I nod to a young mother on one side of me who is holding; you guessed it, a newborn baby. Okay God, I get it. You are not going to let me forget. I'm sorry, okay? On the other side of me, a woman who looks to be about my age fiddles. She tries to find a place for her large purse. She smiles at me.

I like the Pastor. He also looks to be close to my age. I look around and see the congregation is made up of all ages. I like this. One of the things they do at the beginning of the message is to dismiss all the kids to children's church. I've never seen anything so cute. Kids begin to move from every area of the church. Some run, skip and many are holding hands of younger siblings. I think to myself, these kids are the future of a church. I find I enjoy the scene even though guilt still pulses through me.

The pastor begins. Why is it, so often a pastor's message seems to be directed to me? It's like they have a camera focused on my life. He begins to talk about everyday trials. He starts to list money problems, jobs, death and grief, divorce and more. I squirm a little in my seat. I wonder where this is going? Then he says, "Rebuilding after a trial doesn't mean your life goes back to what it was before the incident took place. It just means you try to pick up the pieces of your life and put them together in a different way."

The woman next to me pulls a tissue from her purse. I look at her and see tears run down her cheeks. If I weren't so wrapped up in my own messed up head, I might reach over and grab her hand. Instead, I pull a tissue out of my own purse.

I half listen to the rest of the sermon because I let myself be absorbed in my own self-pity party. Just before I realize the pastor has finished speaking, I hear him say. "I, the Lord am with you and will watch over you wherever you go."

The music pastor asks everyone to stand. This is my opportunity to sneak out quietly. I excuse myself to the young woman with the infant and step in front of her. Of course, I feel like the entire congregation watches me as I head out the back door. By the time I reach my car, I'm in need of a box of tissues. I put Jess's Bible in the passenger's seat and notice a bookmark or a piece of paper has worked its way out of the pages. I pull it out and read, "In God's book, endings are always the preludes to new beginnings."

My head falls forward against the steering wheel. I sense cars moving around me. People stream out of the church. I lean back, put the car into drive and head home.

Chapter Twenty-Nine

Monday morning can't get here fast enough. I spend the rest of Sunday feeling sorry for myself. I also have a conversation with God, but, before I pour my heart out to Him, I stuff Jess's Bible back into the music chest. I want to feel God's presence, I really do. And yes, some good things have happened to me: the move, the Green family and now, maybe some new friends. Oh, and who knows, maybe a modeling career?

***

I walk to the office by way of several of the barns this Monday. The always-sweet smell of fresh hay and wood shavings helps me still feel welcome in the place I'm at right now, with people who care about me.

"Good morning Karen." Lois greets me as I make my way to my desk. "Hope you had a nice weekend. I've left a folder on your desk of the new fillies and colts we need to photograph today and Mr. Green has called a meeting for all staff at two this afternoon."

"Thanks, Lois, and yes my weekend was full. I'll get right on scheduling the photo session with the trainers."

I pass by Mr. Green's office and notice for the first time, there is a beautiful stained glass window along the very top of the ceiling in his office. Must be the sun has just caught it because I haven't noticed it before now. The colors are brilliant with the sun streaming through the glass; reds, blues, bits of orange and a smattering of purple beam in the light. Right in the center are three white crosses.

"Good Morning." Mr. Green comes up behind me. He nods toward the window. "The trinity. My wife had the window installed the year she passed away. She said she wanted me to remember always that she would be with The Father, Son and Holy Spirit when her Lord takes her home to free her of the pain she had as the cancer destroyed her body. I've found it comforts me more than I ever thought could be possible."

I feel Mr. Green's hand on my back. "Jim tells me you two went to Wiley Wranglers on Saturday. We used to love that place. Carolyn could really dance. I only stumbled around the floor with her. I'm glad you are getting out some." He walks past me into his office and taps the end of my nose just like my daddy often does.

"The window is beautiful and yes I had a good time with Jim. The place is sure popular. I'd better get busy. Guess we have a meeting, at two?"

"Yes, we are going to get ready to start the previews and need to do some planning. You will be doing the commentary for the previews and I have full confidence you will do a super job."

I walk to my desk while I let his words settle in my brain. I'm really looking forward to this opportunity. I did so well in college in my speech class and I have never felt fear in front of a crowd.

The day seems to fly by. I feel good about our meeting. We took more than enough photos of the horses, and the trainers and grooms worked well together. The proofs will be ready by the end of the week. Gosh, I love this job.

It's starting to stay light longer. I'm going to take Ibn for a short ride before the sun dips behind the mountain. I'm the last one out of the office, so I lock up and walk home to change into my softer Levi's.

By the time I get to the barn, I see Kent and Jim are just coming back from the stallion area. They both raise their arms and wave. Kent turns his horse and wanders toward the vet lab. Jim comes toward me in a trot. "Going out for a ride?" He tips his hat. "Mind if I ride along?"

"Sure, why not? I thought I'd ride east toward the McDowell Mountains. Seems like there are less homes to weave in and out of. When did this area start building so many houses? Guess it was bound to happen." I wave a hand at him to join me.

"It's only been the last few years that we've seen so many builders. I always thought we'd have the solitude forever out here. I'm glad our ranch is so big. We still feel more or less alone out this far."

Jim nudges his horse Jake into a slow trot. Ibn follows suit. We trot for some time. I marvel at all there is to see in the Arizona desert. It's definitely warming up and the wild yellow poppies cover the ground. The grasshoppers are popping up from the tall grass and Ibn actually lifts his front feet like he's dancing when they fly up at his nose. He has never liked the grasshoppers. I laugh out loud. "Ibn hates the bugs." Jim chuckles.

A long open stretch is in front of us. Jim looks at me and winks before he says, "Hey Jake, let's show Karen how a cowboy rides."

It only takes me a second to accept the challenge. I cue Ibn into a canter and squeeze my heels deep into his side to give him permission to fly like the wind. And fly he does. Within minutes I pass Jake and offer Jim a victory sign. Ibn may be old, but he loves to gallop more than anything. I'm a good five hundred feet in front when I slow Ibn by barely touching the reins with two fingers. Dang, he is so well trained!

Jim rides up beside me. "Okay girl, I stand defeated. I forgot your uncle trained Ibn. I also forgot he used to race him down at the fairgrounds. He is in great shape for an old boy. Congratulations."

I feel a smug sneer move across my face. "Yep, you're right, but I guess I shouldn't ride the old boy so hard." I reach down and stroke the side of Ibn's neck and push his forelock to one side. He gives me a soft snort.

We get back to the ranch and Jim offers to let me stop at my place. "I can take Ibn back to the barn, cool him off and give him some extra oats along with his hay. This way you'll have more of your evening to do whatever beautiful girls do in their spare time."

"My, my, Jim Green, are you flirting with me, a fellow employee?" I feel heat rise up my neck. It threatens to climb to my cheeks.

"No Mrs. Anderson, just telling a truth." He turns and slaps Jake on the behind, gathers Ibn's reins and is off to the barn.

I stand by the front door until he turns a corner and I can no longer see him. I'm surprised how giddy I feel. I wrap my arms around myself to ward off the cool evening and glance at the sunset in the west corner of the ranch. It's wondrous, as are most of the sunsets here in Arizona.

Chapter Thirty

My week is busy and fulfilling. It's already Friday night. I'm home warming some meatloaf from the night before when my cell phone rings.

"Hey Karen, it's me, Sylvia."

"Oh, hi Sylvia, what's up?"

"I was just wondering if you have thought about my proposal? I have a client who is looking for a face for still photo work for a major beauty product and I think you would be perfect for the job. Interested?"

I'm more than taken back at her request. There is a long pause.

"Karen, are you there?"

I swallow and sputter into the phone. "Yes, yes, sorry. I don't know what to say. I guess I need to ask when and where because I work five days a week." I hesitate for a few minutes with the phone down at my side. I lift it to my ear. "Can I ask you why these clients aren't looking at twenty year olds? Aren't I just a bit too old to be doing this?"

"I kind of thought you might ask that question Karen. I have lots of clients who are indeed looking for the pencil thin type model we see in the media, but we also know a more mature look is what sells certain items. So, we hire people from babies to people in their nineties. Whatever works and brings in the dough, if you know what I mean?" I can imagine Sylvia snickering before she continues.

"No problem about weekdays. My client is only here for the weekend and we could meet tomorrow morning for an interview. If he likes you, and I'm certain he will, the photo shoot usually takes several hours. It pays a flat rate and I think it will be worth your while. What do you say?"

I feel lightheaded and am surprised when I hear myself answer. "Sure, why not, time to be adventurous. What time? Yep, I can be there then. Okay then, see you tomorrow." I press the end button on my phone and fall down into the soft folds of my couch cushions.

"What have I done?"

***

I take a long look at my reflection in my bathroom mirror. Thank goodness, I still have a makeup kit full of goodies I used when I worked for Tom. Most of the time, here at the ranch, I just put on a little mascara and I call it all good. I'm careful to dab a little concealer on the shadow under my eyes. Must be because I was awake much of last night thinking about this crazy decision I've made.

My mother always told me one day I would be pleased I had natural curls. The sunlight here in Arizona has tipped the ends of my natural dark gold blond hair almost white. It looks like I had it colored intentionally. I push a curl behind one ear. Gosh, my hair is growing. It's almost to my shoulders now. I finish with a dab of blush on my cheeks and head out the door.

Sylvia's office isn't too far of a drive into downtown Scottsdale from the ranch. I arrive a few minutes early. I pull into the driveway and see Sylvia's sign, "Amazing Grace Agency." Really, I can't imagine how she came by this name.

She greets me at the front door, and explains her staff has Saturday and Sunday off. As she takes my hand, a very tall man walks up behind her. He is dressed casually in a striped blue and tan shirt and tan slacks. His thick black hair is streaked with grey and his lips are closed but definitely turned into a grin.

"Gregory, this is Karen. We are old friends and I think she might be just the ticket for your project. Karen, Gregory." He reaches across Sylvia with his large hand outstretched and takes mine. He winces slightly and cocks his head.

"Wow, now that's a grip Karen. Glad to meet you."

"I'm a little embarrassed, but my daddy taught me to shake hands firmly. No dead fish shakes in our home. Nice to meet you too Gregory."

Sylvia ushers us to her office. Gregory speaks first. "Yes, Sylvia, I like her. I think she will be perfect. She has skin like ivory. Our product and her face are a perfect testimony to the world." He laughs.

I fidget in my seat. I'm not used to compliments like this. I'm sure I'm blushing.

Gregory stands. "Why don't we see what we can do with a few photos?"

Sylvia stands too and we walk down a colorful wall covered with smiling faces of models I assume are part of Sylvia's agency. We enter a stark white room. Professional lights are placed around the edges. On one wall, there is a corner-to-corner pull down contraption. Sylvia walks over and pulls on a cord. "How about we start with a cool mint green background lined with poppies and daisies."

I feel like I am part of an Alice in Wonderland scene. Sylvia opens part of the wall and there is an amazing array of clothing. She reaches in and pulls out a soft yellow dress with a full skirt. The bodice is lace, just a bit lighter yellow than the rest of the dress. Next, she reaches to a shelf above the dresses and brings a large hat out and says, "Yes, this will do. Perfect."

I find out the product is a national, very well known one I actually use. It's a moisturizer and it really does work. At least I think so. The ad will be, then, a national ad in many magazines, fourteen in the United States and three in London. I'm stunned, but excited at the same time.

I change into the dress. Sylvia asks me to sit on the floor before she sets the hat on my head, tilts it back slightly, and arranges the full skirt of the dress across the floor. I must look like I am sitting in a field of flowers. Gregory begins his magic. "Turn your head a bit to the right, now look right at the lens. Good, now tilt your head back and laugh. Yes, let's have some fun. Looking good, Karen. Just relax. Now, put your fingertips on the edge of the hat. Yep. Great. You're a natural."

Chapter Thirty-One

Well, that was quite the experience. I spent three hours at Sylvia's studio and made three hundred dollars. Not bad for a little extra dough! Now she has another client she wants to introduce me to, something about some still photos for another magazine ad. It surely wasn't hard work, if you know what I mean, and the photos looked darn good if I do say so myself. Talk about a little ego boost. Guess I am not such a plain Jane after all. Ha!

I drive down the long lane to the ranch just as night begins to settle a blanket over the sun. The ranch seems quiet. By this time, the horses have been fed and put up for the night. As I turn into my space in front of my cottage, my headlights flash across my front door. It looks like there is a note hanging above the doorknob.

"If you get home before seven, give me a call. Thanks, Jim." I wonder if something is wrong. As soon as I'm inside and put my things down, I call.

"Hey Jim, it's me. Is everything okay? I just got home and saw your note on the door." I turn to find my favorite spot on the couch and sit down. I sense hesitation in Jim's voice.

"Can I come over Karen?"

"Why of course, but I sense something is wrong. Is everyone okay?"

"I'll be right there." My phone is silent.

I get up and turn on the porch light. Now I pace in front of the window. Something is wrong. I know it!

I open the door before Jim has a chance to knock. "What's wrong? Tell me."

His face is blotchy red. He looks at me and before he says a word he grabs me in a tight embrace. "Karen, I'm so sorry."

I push him away. "What do you mean?" I look at his face and know he is about to tell me something horrible. "Tell me."

"It's your mother, Karen. Your dad called my dad because he wanted someone to be with you. Your mother has had a major heart attack. She is on life support and not expected to live. Your dad is at the hospital. He told us to keep you here in Arizona and he would call this evening."

To say ripples of shock run up my spine would be candy coating the emotion hitting me. Jim takes hold of my elbows and backs me to the couch. He sits beside me. I feel absolutely numb. My mouth can't form any words. But then…

"This can't be possible. My mom is a picture of health." I reach for my phone. "I have to call my dad."

Jim puts his arm around my shoulders. "Karen, your dad said to wait for his call. He might not be able to talk if you try him. How about we go to my house. My family is gathered there and we want to be your support team. Please Karen?"

I feel nothing. I can't even cry. I find myself standing and Jim gently guides me toward the front door and out into the now still darkness of night.

***

The phone finally rings. "Daddy? Is Mom okay?" I sense a much too long pause.

Daddy clears his throat. "No Karen, your mother has passed." I hear a catch in his throat and I know he is crying.

"Daddy, how did this happen? Mom has been the healthy one in our family. I must come home. I'll get the first plane out in the morning." I let my own tears fall. Daddy and I cry together while the entire Green family wraps their arms around me. I hand the phone to Mr. Green. Jim, once again, guides me to sit down. Jim, Kent, and Phyllis surround me.

I hear Mr. Green talking to my dad. "Yes, Paul, I will take care of it. Don't you worry. Yes, we will keep her in the main house tonight. All right, please let us know when you've made all the arrangements. We are so very sorry and will be praying for you."

***

Why, why do these things happen? I hardly remember the rest of the evening at the Green's. I find myself waking in a strange bed in the morning. When I look at my face in the bathroom mirror, I can see I must have cried in my sleep. Dried mascara is in streaks down my cheeks and my eyeballs are beet red.

I smell coffee brewing. I wash my face. Lavender, the soap I use, it's my mother's favorite smell. Then it hits me again. My mother is gone. Just like Jess, gone. I panic. I must make plane arrangements. Where's my phone? I search the nightstand. I slept in my clothes and I can't find my phone. I open the door and rush down a flight of stairs. I'm not sure where I'm going. I must be at the Green's.

Just as I get to the landing at the end of the stairs, Mr. Green walks toward me with a steaming cup of coffee. "Ah, I thought I heard you."

I pass right by him. "Have you seen my phone? I need to get a plane ticket home. Where's my phone?"

"Whoa, little one. First of all, I have taken care of the plane ride home and the earliest I could get you on is three-thirty this afternoon. It is only six-thirty in the morning, you have lots of time. Come on now; let's go to the kitchen." He steps toward me, hands me the coffee cup and wraps an arm around my shoulder.

Kent and Jim are already at the table. Phyllis is at the sink rinsing some plates and Jacob is on the floor pushing a small tractor under the chair legs. The men get up from the table. "Morning, Karen." They say in unison and then look at each other and sit down.

I take a sip of my coffee. I feel like I'm going to cry, but hold the tears at bay. "Hi guys. Thank you for taking me in, everyone. I feel really blessed to have all of you in my corner."

Jim pulls a chair out. "Here, please Karen. You know we are all here for you. Just name it, it'll be done." His eyes search mine. And Kent nods in my direction.

Mr. Green sits next to me. He has a piece of paper in his hands. "I took the liberty of printing your boarding pass,

Karen. We'll get you to the airport and your dad will be picking you up. Once arrangements are made, the rest of us will be in Texas to support you." He touches the tip of his forehead with a two-finger salute and squeezes my hand.

"I don't know what to say. You are all so amazing." Tears slip and trickle down my face. "Can any of you give me an answer as to why this has happened? Why is God doing this to me?" My head falls forward and I let go of my built-up grief as I bury my face in my arms on the tabletop.

Chapter Thirty-Two

I look out the airplane window and I reflect on the answers the Green family gave me when I asked them to make sense of this. Jim quickly said, "I'm not sure God caused anything. I know He knows His plan for each of us. At the same time, Karen, people eat wrong, some smoke, others don't exercise, or gain weight and health suffers. I just know God loves us all unconditionally and something, some lesson can be learned from trial."

Kent butted in. "All of us are going to die. In the end, we will know all the answers, when we are all together again in God's kingdom. I know that sounds so sterile and as if I don't care, but I do Karen, we all do. We all hurt for you and for ourselves. We lost a dear friend, and much too early..."

"Yes," Phyllis said. "The guys are right, we are all going to grieve. Your mom was a wonderful woman. We will miss her, but we also know we will indeed see her again. And yes, we are sad. It hurts."

I scrunch my shoulders and look at the clouds. They seem to float around us as the plane makes its way to Texas. Oh Jess, please take care of my mom. She used to say you were her dream come true for me. What will my daddy do? We don't have any family living in Texas. Maybe I'll have to move back.

"This is your captain speaking. We are a few minutes shy of our descent. The weather in Texas is its usual balmy humid self." He laughs. "At least there is a breeze and no sign of rain."

I find myself smiling. We touch down on the runway, taxi to a stop and since I'm close to the front, excitement to see my dad flutters in my chest. The guy seated in front of me offers to retrieve my carryon bag. I thank him and make my way out of the plane.

My dad stands tall off to the right in the waiting area. I want to run to him but a couple of older ladies are taking their time in front of me. Instead, I raise my free hand and wave to him.

When I reach him, Dad wraps me in his arms and I feel my feet leave the ground as he picks me up and buries his chin into my neck. "Oh, my sweet daughter. I have missed you."

"I missed you too Daddy." I tell myself not to cry when I see my dad, but guess that didn't work, because when I pull my face from his shoulder, I see my tears have left a big blotch of wet on his blue shirt.

We exit the airport quickly. Dad starts to talk about the arrangements for a memorial service. Mother only wanted a celebration of life service. She used to say, "I don't want people looking at me when I'm dead."

When we reach the house, my stomach churns.

The house seems unusually quiet. Daddy and I sit at the kitchen table. He makes us a cup of tea. My mom preferred tea to coffee and I guess Daddy has picked up the habit. My eyes search for sight of my mom. Everything in the house is her; the lilac's that sit in the window above the sink. They need more water and the neatly folded towels we are never supposed to use because they are for 'show' only, and the floor beneath us, which gleams with a fresh shine.

"I don't know what to say, Daddy. Was Mom sick and you didn't tell me or what?" Dad sits next to me after delivering our tea to the table. "No honey, not sick, nothing. We had just come in from grocery shopping. I carried all the bags. She put her purse on the counter and the next thing I knew, she fell to the floor. No warning."

"Daddy." I take his hands. "It must have been horrible for you. I'm so sorry I wasn't here. How awful for you."

"This may sound crazy but I knew she was not going to stay with me. I don't understand it, but I felt a peace. I know that sounds nuts. You know we believe in God, but we have never been crazy religious, like regularly going to church, but I knew right then if she died, she would be in heaven." His eyes search mine.

It's all too much. I lay my head on the table and sob. Daddy rubs my back. "It's okay, it's okay. We can do this."

Dad tells me he has already contacted Pastor Rodney. He says Pastor Rodney is the only pastor he knows. He is grateful he met him at my wedding. I shake my head. I guess it will be a reunion of sorts. My first call is to my children, I know it will be hard for them to get away, mainly because of their work schedules and finances. They sure loved Mom and I know she would understand if they can't be here.

Debee and Bill will come to the service. Gosh, Debee is almost due to deliver her baby. It will be good to see them. I should also call my old boss Tom. He knew my mom.

Dad goes to bed early and I make some phone calls. Debee is excited to hear from me and obviously shocked to hear why I call her. Tom is stunned but also anxious to give his regards and have a chance to visit with me. It will be a small service. I guess I need to call some of the ladies Mom played bridge with and maybe her knitting club as well. None of this seems real.

***

The next morning, we are off to the funeral home to make last minute arrangements. I feel strange because I can't see Mom. She was cremated, her wish. Dad picks out an urn; we talk about flowers and food.

We pick up Mexican food on the way home. I set the table and we eat in silence.

"Daddy, do you want me to move back to Texas? You know, I can help around the house. Tom would give me my job..."

"Absolutely not, Karen." Dad leaps up from the table and runs his fingers through his graying hair. "I'm not an invalid, you know. I will be just fine."

"Oh, Dad, I know that. I just thought we could kind of watch out for each other. Please sit back down. Maybe you might consider moving back to Arizona. You could bunk with me. Aunt Mary is there too and you love the ranch. It will be like old times."

"Yeah, without your mother. No, I don't think so." He almost spits the words at me.

"Just think about it, please. I would love to have you live with me. We could make a great team. I bet Mr. Green could find something to keep you busy around the ranch. I know the roses sure need your attention." I lay my hand on top of his. "Just think about it, okay?"

***

The service is perfect. It's very small but some of Mom's lady friends make great efforts to show their support. The knitting group brings a beautiful afghan depicting all of Mom's favorite flowers. The bridge group wears red hats. I forgot Mom was a Red Hatter. Debee and Bill sit on one side of me and the whole Green family is spread out behind us. Aunt Mary sits beside Dad, her arm linked through his. Aunt Mary and the Greens all came in just for the day and will be leaving later after the service.

Jim pulls me aside at the reception. "Karen, is there anything I can do? I can stay on if you want me too. The rest of the family has to get back to run the ranch but I really can stay if you need some help." His blue eyes appear deep with concern.

"I'm still a little numb, Jim. I don't know right now what I need. It's sweet of you to offer. I'm going to try and convince Daddy to move back to Arizona. I want him to move in with me. There is no one here for him. Just give me a couple of weeks."

Mr. Green comes behind me. "I heard that Karen. You can take all the time you need. There is nothing pressing because it's starting to get hot at home and our business doesn't pick up until around September. Take your time. I'd love to have Paul at the ranch." He hugs me and quickly walks to where my father is standing with other guests.

"See?" Jim grabs my hands in his. "So, what do you say?"

***

I make sure Jim understands that I think I can handle things from this point forward. I pile the whole gang in Dad's suburban to see they are at the airport well before their flight takes off. There is a lot of "I love you" and reassurance they are all on my side.

On the way back to the house, I feel surprisingly content. I feel Mom looking down on me, I'm sure she is happy the service was simple. Then it hits... my anger returns. She's gone, really gone. Why? I try so hard to recount the conversation about trust with Pastor Rodney. I try to visualize scripture I've read and I draw blanks. I don't see or feel any hope.

Chapter Thirty-Three

It's almost time for me to go back to Arizona. I've been here nearly two weeks. Dad and I have had some wonderful talks and he has agreed the move to Arizona might be good for him. I'm really excited. Dad has always been my hero. Mom was certainly a good mother, but we were never connected like so many of my girlfriends used to tell me they were with their moms. I've always loved to do all the outdoor things with my dad: sports, fishing and hunting. Oh, and camping too. Mom hated bugs. She would never have slept in a tent.

We're going to drive to Arizona together. One of Dad's neighbors bought the house for one of his daughters. We are leaving most of the furniture and even the dishes and stuff we don't have any need for. I told Dad to dust off his old pair of boots because I want him to ride with me once we are settled in at the ranch. We laughed when he tried to shove his feet into his boots. We throw them in the garbage. Looks like a trip to the boot barn in Arizona will be necessary!

I sit on the front porch swing, a place Mom used to love to sit, and watch Dad prune his roses. I can't believe so many trials have taken place this past year. I'm beginning to feel older than my almost forty-three years.

"Hi sweetheart." My dad climbs the porch steps and settles in beside me. "Lot's on your mind, huh?" He pats my hands and pulls one to his lips for a kiss. "You've had more happen to you in just short of a year than most have in a lifetime."

"I guess so Daddy. Do you really think God is in control of our lives? Do you think He gives us what we can handle? Have you made any sense of this?"

"You're asking me?" Dad laughs, then props his feet on the porch rail in front of the swing. "I doubt I am qualified to answer your questions honey. I'm a believer. Mom too. I mean, we believe in the trinity, but I don't know if I am qualified to answer your questions. I've read some scripture in my day and funny you bring this up." He bends forward to get his backside off the seat and pulls a pocket Bible from his jeans. He starts to read.

"Blessed is the man who perseveres under trial, because when he has stood the test, he will receive the crown of life that God has promised to those who love him." Dad keeps his finger between the pages, looks at me, lifts my chin and continues. "I don't know the answers Karen. I don't think any of us do. But, I do have faith that Mom and I will see each other again. Comfort? Not really at this minute. However, I do believe in God and I believe some good will be learned from each trial we face. So there, do I sound like a preacher?" He ruffles the top of my head with his knuckles.

I can't believe this is my dad. I honestly had no idea he read the Bible. I fall across his lap and let loose a torrent of tears which cause me to hiccup and wail. Daddy rubs my shoulders and back until I stop. I straighten up. "Thank you, Daddy. I can actually say I feel better and it sure feels good to listen to you. You always seem to know how to make me feel better even if I don't want to agree with you."

"Well, I don't know about that, but I do know we need to get something to eat, pack the rest of our belongings and get a good night's sleep before we take off tomorrow. What do you say, Mexican food again?"

***

Morning sun wakes me before I begin to take in the fact Dad and I will leave for Arizona... without Mom. I roll over to step out of bed and I catch my reflection in the mirrored closet door. My hair is finally getting some length on it and I quickly stand and grab it with my hand toward the nape of my neck. I also realize I look a little thin. Must be all the stress. I shower, dress and meet Dad, who is already having his last cup of coffee in a home he shared with his wife of many years.

"Morning Dad, I just need a cup of coffee and a piece of toast and I'm ready to go. I packed us a lunch last night before I went to bed. I also folded the bed sheets and will stuff them in the suburban. I think the place is ready for the new owner." I brush my hands along Dad's shoulder and kiss him on top his head.

"Great, I'm ready too. I'll rinse the coffeepot and tuck it in the back seat. Arizona, here we come." Dad has one of his straw hats laying on his knee, the one he uses when he gardens. He picks it up and places it on his head. He scoots the chair under the table, tips the straw hat and a grin spreads across his face. "Meet you outside then."

I rinse my coffee cup, dry it and put it in the cupboard. I finish my toast, scrape the crumbs off the table and put them down the garbage disposal. I take one last look through the house. I know the young daughter who is going to live here will be blessed. I holler through the screen door to Dad. "Coming." I feel the door snap to a lock when I pull the key out and place it in our secret place for the new owner.

Chapter Thirty-Four

The entire Green family waits for us at the end of the tree-lined lane. I point to the mares in the field. "Look Dad, at all the mares and their babies. This is what soothes my soul on a daily basis." Some of the mares raise their heads and whinny. The babies are getting so big. Some of them leave the safety of their mothers to trot alongside the fence as we make our way to our group of greeters.

Mr. Green is the first to open the suburban door to welcome Dad. "Great to see you again, Paul, and welcome." He points to the roses lining the office walls. "I told you we have lots of work piled up for you." He pulls Dad into a bear hug before he is entirely out of the car.

The rest of the gang offer more hugs and good wishes. I feel a little left out. "Hey, where are my hugs?" I whine. Little Jacob almost flies through the air before he plows into my legs. I'm really surprised and stagger a little. I don't know what comes over me, but I stoop down and pick him up. "Hey there buddy, thanks for the hugs." His eyes open wide and he squirms to get down." Something stabs at my insides.

"You're welcome," he shouts as he runs back to Phyllis's arms.

Jim walks toward me with his arms outstretched. "Well now it's my turn. Welcome home." He pulls me into his arms in a tight embrace. I say, 'embrace,' because the hug feels just a little too tight. I realize he's going to kiss me. I turn my head in time for the kiss to land on my cheek.

"Thank you, everyone." I bow at the waist. "Now, if you will allow us to get to the cottage to unwind…"

The loud honking of a horn startles me. It's Aunt Mary. She has her arm out the window, waving like a mad woman. She parks and hugs everyone, starting with Dad. "I thought I'd be here on time to see you drive up but one of the mares has a twisted gut." She waves a hand in the air. "Oh, she is good now. No worries. Doc Jones got there just in time." She takes a deep breath. "You all get settled. I brought chili and cornbread and two of my key lime pies, enough for the whole gang."

I feel my shoulders slump. Is anyone else so lucky to have all these people in their lives? We finish small talk. I take Dad to the cottage. Someone has put a bouquet of flowers on the table and a big fruit basket sits on the kitchen counter. I shake my head. "You see, Daddy, can you believe these people?"

"It's pretty obvious you are well taken care of. I think I'm going to love living here." Dad gives me a hug. He taps my nose. "Do I get the master bedroom?" He laughs one of those laughs, which fills my heart with peace. I'm sure I made a good decision by encouraging him to move in with me.

While Dad is cleaning up, I flip the television on. The PBS station is showing a taping of some sort of fund raising event. Just as I turn up the sound on the television, I see Stevie Wonder sitting at the piano. He starts to play, "I Just Called To Say I Love you." The words grab at my heart. It's so strange the way this song filters into my life. Then, I remember how Jim told me the song is one of his favorite songs, too. Hmmm. I sit deep into the couch's leather. I feel compelled to pray, something I'm not doing much of lately. "Please let me know somehow, that good will come even from these recent trials. Please guide me."

I hear my phone beep. I reach across the end table to check who might be sending me a message. It's Jim. He posts a smiley face and hearts. "Dinner will be served in twenty minutes. Come to Kent's house. Dad says his kitchen is a mess. LOL."

Dad comes out of his bedroom. "Is that our dinner bell? Guess I'm going to have to get one of them smart phones. My old flip phone must really be out of date." He pulls his phone out of his shirt pocket.

"Goodness Daddy, that phone is ancient!" I make sure I roll my eyes. "And yes, Jim says we should meet at Kent's place. You will love Phyllis. She is so sweet and it's obvious she and Kent are in love. Do you think I will ever fall in love again Daddy?" I reach for another one of his hugs.

"My precious daughter, of course you will. I know Jess would want that for you. You know it too. Don't you?"

I nod toward the front door. "Yes, I suppose I do."

Chapter Thirty-Five

It's already closing in on September. I
have no idea where the months went. So
many changes in my life; a new type of life
now at the ranch, Aunt Mary, the Green
family, Mom gone and Dad here, and now we
are getting ready for the previews at the
ranch to really keep me busy.

The colts and fillies are weaned, and
many mares re-bred in order to go in the
sales in January. Grooms are polishing coats,
painting hooves and readying the sales
horses for the previews. I've become efficient
with a camera, prepared all the pedigrees
and studied the history of the Arabian horse.

My dad fits right in with the Green
family and he and Aunt Mary have become
good friends. They often play cards in the
evenings and enjoy reminiscing about some
of Mom's antics when she and Aunt Mary
were little. The roses by the office are kept
pruned, watered and cared for by Dad. Mr.
Green remarks nearly every day about how
they are flourishing.

I really believe Jim's crush on me is
somewhat obvious. Almost every week, he
asks me for dinner, dancing or a movie. I

enjoy his company. He makes me laugh. I sometimes feel like he is more like one of my girlfriends, because I'm able to talk to him about my feelings, good or bad. He has a good listening ear. He keeps telling me I should try dating. I tell him he must be crazy, that I am not ready. He laughs and insists the grooms on the ranch have the hots for me. Get real, I tell him.

My birthday is this week and Jim has asked to take me to dinner to celebrate. I feel a lot older than soon to be forty-three. I think about turning fifty soon. Jess was only forty-three. Quit it Karen.

I look at my watch. Jim will be here any minute. I take a peek at myself in the hall mirror. I have my hair pulled back into a high ponytail. Small wisps of curl frame my cheeks; the pieces still too short to stay back. I'm wearing a new pair of colored jeans, pale blue, and a cobalt blue shirt. My new boots have a trail of blue butterflies along the side arch. There's the doorbell.

Jim stands at the door once again with a handful of flowers he just picked from the garden in front of my cottage. I can't count the number of times he has done this. "Why thank you, Jim. How ever do you find such beautiful flowers?" I reach out and poke him in the shoulder and laugh! "Let me put them in water and I'll be right out."

Jim has the truck door open. As I approach, he takes his hat off and bows. Then he sweeps his hat toward the truck. "At your service, birthday girl."

Jim starts the truck. The radio is already on and yep, you guessed it, Stevie the wonder man starts to sing.

I shake my head. Okay God, what is it with this song? I strap myself in and Jim sings along. He is so dang cute with his cowboy hat tipped off to one side. Did I mention he sports a neatly trimmed mustache? I think he might look about twelve without one.

We get to the restaurant. I'm shocked to find out Jim has made reservations at one of the most expensive in town. I wonder if I'm dressed properly. I thought we were going to one of our regular hangouts, always good to wear jeans and boots.

I'm relieved to see most people are dressed casually. We get situated at a table toward the back. Jim takes complete control by ordering a bottle of wine and a five-course dinner. "Whoa, Jim, this is really very special. Thank you."

"My pleasure, princess. They have a dance floor in the bar. While we wait for dinner, do you want to check it out? I doubt they play Country Western music but I'm sure we can learn something new or just watch." He looks directly at me. His blue eyes seem to soften.

We move to the bar area. The band has just started to play. Can you guess? I bet Jim requested the song. We step to the dance floor where Jim gathers me in his arms like he has done this forever. A slow dance, I can't remember when I danced a slow dance. Might have been at my senior prom. In minutes I find my head resting against Jim's cheek.

"You know, don't you Karen, that I will always have your back? I'll be waiting, if and when you are ready to go on with your life." All of a sudden just as the lead singer sings, "And I mean it from the bottom of my heart," Jim swings me out and twirls me in a circle.

As we walk back to our table, my hands shake and I'm not sure I won't fall. "Excuse me Jim, I need to go to the little girl's room." I turn to make my way to the restroom; my heart drums inside my chest. I look into the mirror. Oh golly, did this just happen. He really does care about me and not in a brotherly way. What should I say?

When I return, I see our salads have been delivered. Jim sits with his hands folded in his lap. He reminds me of a little boy who waits for permission to eat. "Sorry, you shouldn't wait for me." I sit and pick up my fork. Jim reaches over and takes my hand.

"Heavenly Father, thank you for this evening with a special friend. Thank you for the food prepared for us. May it nourish us. In Jesus's name, amen."

I feel foolish once again for not remembering Jim always says grace before a meal. Of course, he would wait for me. Why do I still feel so uncomfortable? Jim prays at every meal; prayer is part of his life...

I stammer. "I have to, to ask you Jim, do you think I will ever be able to find comfort in God again?" Tears threaten to confirm what a crybaby I am. One tear drops to my chin when I raise my head. Jim reaches across the table to wipe another from my cheek.

I'm not only feeling anger toward God but the guilt I harbor in my heart about not wanting my baby and knowing I must surely be the cause of my miscarriage makes me want to push back from this table and run, just run from life. My silence is broken when Jim interrupts my thoughts.

"Karen, I do know how hard it is to accept the trials we are handed in life. I also know, absolutely, that God is patient. I don't have answers for you and I can't wave a magic wand to heal your heart. But I can let you know how much I care about you and I'm willing to give you all the time you need to consider a life with me."

A dam breaks in my heart just as the main course is set before us. I'm shocked at his words. Jim hands a napkin to me and then motions to the waiter to pour the wine.

Jim lifts his glass for a toast. "Here's to a bright future for a very lovely lady and here's to a very happy birthday to remind her she is loved by a whole gang of people."

I'm sure I blush when several of the waiters and waitresses come to the table and start singing, "Happy birthday to you." I always thought they did this when they brought dessert, so I'm really embarrassed.

I hold my glass up once more and tip it toward Jim and silently mouth the words, "Thank you."

While we sit at the table and enjoy our meal, I hear a beep come from my phone. I glance at it, trying to do so inconspicuously. I see it's a text message from Sylvia. I recognize the agency's number. Since there is a lull in our conversation, I decide to tell Jim about my modeling session.

I swallow a bite of food. "Oh, by the way, did I tell you about meeting an old high school friend who has a modeling agency?"

"Yep, but I don't think I asked you if I know her?"

"I don't think so. She went to college with me and only one year. Anyway, last weekend I went to her studio and did an ad printout for a cosmetic product. It was really simple and almost fun. I think the copy comes out next month in several magazines."

"Wow, really Karen? That's great. Didn't I tell you, you're more than a pretty face?" He sits back in his chair and ducks his head in a bow. "I rest my case."

"Well, I don't think I'm going to get rich off of it, so don't tell your dad. I love my job. I rest my case!" Now we both enjoy a symphony of laughter.

Our evening goes by fast and I really do enjoy myself. Jim is so easy to be with. When he walks me to my cottage, he leans over and picks a single red rose from a bush by the front door. "Ouch!" He licks the end of his finger. "That thing reached out and bit me."

"I think maybe you deserve it, you know, stealing from my bushes!" More laughter. I give him a strong hug. I whisper. "Thanks for a wonderful evening. I really am grateful for your friendship."
He hugs me back. "And I, for yours, Karen. Remember what I said. I'm a pretty patient guy." He tips his hat and turns to get in his truck.

Chapter Thirty-Six

The next morning before I head for the office, I call Sylvia. The phone rings once. "Hey Karen, glad you called me back so quick. I have an amazing opportunity for you. One of my clients saw the prints of the session you did last week and wants your face for a national product. Only thing is the shoot takes place in New York. All your expenses will be paid. We can even fit it in on a weekend so you don't have to take off work. What do you say?"

My head reels. She spouts so much in a few minutes I'm not sure I hear everything she says. "Whoa, Sylvia. Back up. You talk so fast I'm not sure I got everything. Plus, are you really serious? Why me?"

"Sorry, Karen and yes I'm serious. It's for a moisturizer and a famous photographer in New York will photograph you. The ad printout will be in major magazines, even well known magazines in Europe. If you want to come over this evening, we can solidify the details."

The pause seems extra-long before I finally sputter, "I, I don't know. This just seems crazy. I guess I need a few minutes to think about it. Can I call you back after I get

off work tonight? Sylvia agrees and I hurry
to finish dressing for work.

***

New York, here I come. I sit on the
airplane and question how all of this came
about. Look at all these things popping into
my life. Are these things taking place
because I need distractions from my pity
parties? The attention is sure not doing
anything for all the guilt I feel. Should I be
enjoying all this attention? I haven't even
asked for forgiveness for so much wrong in
my life. Jess must be rolling on the ground in
heaven. I ran away after Jess's death. I
helped abort my own flesh and blood and
don't even think about it when I'm so
involved in the ranch and now this. Maybe
I'm just destined for hell and I shouldn't
worry about it. Just listen to you, Karen,
feeling so sorry for yourself.

I push my head into the backrest of
my seat and gaze out the window of the
plane. The sky, so blue, is laced with wispy
clouds. I form the words in my head. Okay,
God, here I am most likely closer to you than
when I'm on land. I'm really so troubled over
the loss of my baby. I have to say, and you
know I didn't want the baby. I know I was
wrong to ride Ibn so hard. I'm not going to

church; I haven't picked up a Bible in forever. I know I need to ask for your forgiveness. I know this. I just don't know if one can be forgiven for not feeling.

I must have fallen asleep because the flight attendant shakes my shoulder. "Please return your seat to an upright position. Thank you." She moves on to the next row.

The plane is about to land. Seat belts are snapped in place. My mind switches to the task in front of me. I've never been outside of Arizona or Texas. I feel a little nervous. Sylvia told me to look for a cab and give directions to the hotel I'd be staying at Friday and Saturday night, then home on Sunday.

As I walk out of the airport terminal to the street, a man with a ponytail greets me. His shirt opens to his navel. Gold chains adorn his neck and wrists.

"You need transportation lady?"

"Uh, yes. A cab?"

Sneering, he says. "Heck, I have a limo. It will only cost you twenty bucks."

I honestly don't know what comes over me. "Well, okay. That sounds fair."

I follow the man through a garage full of cars to a parked black limo. He opens the door. To my surprise, two people already sit in the back seat. A woman in a business suit nods at me. The other passenger, with pierced lips and eyelids, and covered in tattoos, ignores me completely.

The driver informs me he needs to wait for two more people before we leave. Two well-dressed gentlemen join us. It's obvious to me now why the ride can be offered so cheap. I settle into my seat for the ride.

After the cab driver delivers the other passengers to their destinations and now in route to my hotel, he stops the limo. I feel a moment of panic. I hold my large canvas tote bag, which contains everything I need for my trip, close to my side. As the driver proceeds to get out of the car and approach the backseat, my back stiffens. The thought crosses my mind that I might have to use my bag as a weapon. He reaches for the back door handle and whispers to me when the door opens. "Excuse me lady, but it's been a long day. I need a smoke." He puts his hand into the side panel of my door, pulls out a baggie, shuts the door, and then slides back into the front seat. I watch him roll something into small papers, lick the sides with his tongue, and light an end. I cough. I settle back in my seat. I wonder; can I get high inhaling this stuff swirling through the air?

I tip the driver after we finally arrive at the hotel. I start toward the entrance. The next thing I know, I face the street where I just came from. I really feel stupid when I realize I just walked through revolving doors without getting into the hotel. Thank goodness no one witnessed this unsophisticated bumpkin who doesn't know how to go through a revolving door. On the second try, I make it into the lobby.

It's now eleven thirty at night in New York. The desk clerk checks me in. He asks, "May I call a bellman for your luggage?"

I look up from signing all the paperwork. "Oh, no thank you. I don't have any bags."

The clerk stops writing on the forms, raises his eyebrows and says quietly, "I see."

As I ride the elevator to the fifth floor, I laugh out loud. It dawns on me the clerk thought I could be a "lady of the night." After all, I checked in alone, with no luggage ... I think it might have looked a little suspicious.

Chapter Thirty-Seven

I close the door to my room and promptly snap four locks into place. I run to the window to make sure a fire escape trails to the ground, just in case I need one. The window appears to be nailed shut. I shudder. Visions of gangsters pop into my mind. Without taking my clothes off, I stretch across a squeaky bed. I stare at the ceiling; it needs paint.

Clanking water pipes wake me in the morning. I guess this is common in old hotels. The advertising agency I need to report to told me to come to their office with clean, blown dry hair. I take a quick shower, blow dry my hair, and prepare to dress. I discover while I search through my bag that I forgot to pack extra undergarments. I simply pull my Levi's on without. I put on my slightly wrinkled shirt; check my brushed teeth and head downstairs for breakfast.

Eighteen dollars for one egg, toast, and a cup of coffee seems steep to me. Next, I approach the desk clerk to ask for directions to the advertising agency. He tells me to turn left at the first light and watch for my destination a few blocks away.

There are so many people coming toward me at this hour of the morning I think I've turned onto a one-way only sidewalk, so I turn around. Minutes later, I realize some people indeed walk to the left. I promptly make an about-face and let laughter well up inside me. Who ever heard of a one-way walk?

The red tape I go through after I find the agency makes me feel important. A clerk hands me a badge before he escorts me to an elevator. It takes me to the offices and my contact. I shake hands with a Miss Andrews. She asks me to sign some legal papers before we head back downstairs to a waiting cab.

I know nothing about taxicabs. The minute we leave the curb, our driver begins to scream out the rolled-down window at every passing car. He balls his fists and waves them out the window. The language he spews from his mouth convinces me I need to sit back and leave the driving to him.

We pull up to an ordinary drab building. I expected something a bit fancier. My agent refers to the building as a Brownstone. She opens the door. She nods and directs me to enter ahead of her. An impressive sight lies in front of me. Antique furniture graces the entry and pictures of famous movie stars line the walls. I'm instantly in awe to see the man, who is about to photograph me, is really world famous.

My agent ushers me to a room full of mirrors. She introduces me to a flamboyant gentleman who waves his hands in the air in greeting and sits me in a chair. He is going to be in charge of my makeup and hair. The minute I sit down, he starts my transformation. He places huge rollers in my hair and delicately applies his makeup magic on my face. When he finishes, he turns my chair to face the mirrors. I gasp out loud before I turn my head from side to side. Is this me? Where is MY nose? I'm not kidding. I hardly recognize me.

Another attendant hands me a magnificent pale blue gown. Then places a pair of heavy gold earrings in my right hand. She asks me to be very careful with the dress and earrings because, she says, "They are worth thousands of dollars." I stand still. I feel my eyes flutter. I scan the room. Where could the dressing room be? The attendant looks at me and her eyebrows peek. She says, "You can get dressed now."

Four men glance in my direction. I freeze, my mind races. Here, right here, you want me to undress and put this dress on? (Remember my dilemma when I put my jeans on in the hotel room?)

"Do you have a restroom I might use first?" I rush through the doorway the attendant points to. I lean against the closed door and chuckle at my shy behavior. I guess

I have a lot to learn about this modeling stuff.

As soon as I successfully change, another attendant leads me to the photographers' domain. Bright lights nearly blind me. Several bored looking men with cameras casually lean against the walls of the room. A rather short stout older woman approaches with a powder puff in her right hand. She signals me to sit on the floor. She proceeds to spread my gown across the tile with her fingers. She prods my hair and puffs my chest and neck with powder.

Suddenly, a small framed, bald gentleman who wears dark glasses bursts past a partition. Everyone in the room snaps to attention. The man holds a tiny dog under his left arm. Bright pink colored ribbons peek out from behind the dog's ears. The men holding the cameras hand them, one at a time, to the famous photographer. In a matter of fifteen minutes the entire shoot ends.

After I change into my own clothes, my agent asks me to meet her at the Plaza Hotel for lunch. She tells me she needs to attend to a few things before she can join me. She sketches a small map to show me how to get to the hotel via a short walk. I take a few steps outside when suddenly a torrential rain starts to fall. Buildings in Manhattan don't have overhangs, so, by the time I arrive at the hotel, my drenched clothes stick to my skin. The thick layer of makeup on my face runs down my cheeks. Black mascara makes its way to the corners of my mouth.

When I walk into the elaborate lobby of the Plaza Hotel, I imagine the snooty looking people I pass must think I'm a vagrant. I hurry to a bathroom. My jeans chafe my legs. I remove my blouse and squeeze the water out over a toilet in a stall. I take the blouse to the sink area and blow it dry with the hand blower. Thank goodness no one else comes in. Next, I try to repair the damage to my face, find a hair tie in my purse and slick my hair back into a ponytail. After sitting in wet jeans, I'm grateful the lunch with my agent is brief. We say our goodbyes.

My schedule is supposed to include another night in New York. I find a pay phone in the lobby of the hotel. I change my flight home to leave within a few hours. Goodbye, New York. I'm done with this so-called glamorous trip to a big city.

I've never hailed a cab in my life. At least thirty people stand outside under the protection of the hotel entrance. Rain pounds the streets. I huddle against the building, cold and wet. I feel like the actress in the movie, "The Out of Towner's." What can possibly happen next? I pray silently; Please help me God. Since God hasn't been very important in my life lately, He most likely laughs at my plea…except that He is faithful even when I am not.

A distinguished looking gentleman approaches me. He wears a light grey suit with a matching overcoat and carries an umbrella. A black hat tipped back at an angle on his head makes him look regal. I, on the other hand, must look like a scared, drowned rat. He walks right up to me and asks, "Do you need a cab miss?"

I feel a chill in my spine, probably from my still damp clothes. "Yes sir, I need a cab to the airport."

We start a conversation and within minutes my entire sob story spills from my mouth. He politely listens before he says. "Let me help you. I live here. I know the staff. You just sit tight."

The gentleman opens his umbrella and ducks under it. He walks directly to a bellman in the street. He bends over to whisper something in the man's ear. The bellman becomes energized. He starts to flap his arms like a bird. Minutes later, the kind gentleman waves his hand in an urgent manner for me to come to the curb. He opens the door to a cab and tips his hat. I thank him profusely. As we drive away, I look back to see the throng of people waving their fists in the air. They scream obscenities at my cab. They aren't very happy. I realize the flapping arms from the bellman indicated to a cab driver that a ride to the airport was needed. I'm sure God sent an angel to me this day. Maybe He is taking pity on me since I tried to talk to Him on the airplane on the way here.

Chapter Thirty-Eight

The plane touches down at Sky Harbor Airport. I'm so relieved to be home. The long flight gave me a chance to really think about this new opportunity I've embraced. I've only experienced two sessions and even though I enjoy all the fuss, I feel a little awkward. I'm going to take more time before saying yes to one of Sylvia's offers in the future.

We taxi to an arrival gate. Jim texts me, "I'm here to pick you up. Can't wait to see you."

I surprise myself because I take a few minutes to apply lipstick and run a comb through my hair before I get off the plane. Who am I trying to impress? As I walk into the waiting area, I see Jim standing close to the exit. He waves a bouquet of flowers in the air. Yep, you guessed it, flowers from the garden in front of my cottage. I smile.

Jim pulls me into a hug. He is following in his father's footsteps because the hug is definitely a bear-type hug.

"Gosh I missed you. Did you have a good time? What's it like in New York? Here, let me take your carryon." He snaps the bag from my hand.

"Whoa there, cowboy. Too many questions and I've only been gone two days." I step alongside him and push my arm through his.

"I'll tell you all about it when we are in the truck." We walk and chat non-stop to the parking garage.

Once again, when we begin to drive away, I hear Stevie singing what I'm beginning to believe is my personal song. I start to mention how I feel to Jim when he says, "By the way, I just bought the Stevie Wonder album. I know you love this album, so I thought we might as well be able to hear it whenever we want." He pushes that stubborn lock of hair out of his eyes.

"Great idea Jim. Maybe I can borrow it sometime?"

"You bet, in fact you can take it when we get to the ranch." Jim reaches to turn the volume up. We both laugh and start singing out loud. We sound pretty darn good as a duet!

***

After Jim takes me home and leaves, I open Jess's music chest. His Bible still sits on top of the music. I get into my pajamas, tuck my feet up under me on the couch and open the Bible to Job. Jess often talked about how Job lost so much, yet remained faithful. First I read in the forward, "We must courageously accept what God allows to happen in our lives and remain firmly committed to him." Then, "Don't let any experience drive a wedge between you and God."

Have I placed a wedge between God and me because of Jess's death, or is the wedge there because of the guilt I harbor over my ended pregnancy? I feel another chill creep up my spine, and this time I'm completely numb.

Since I'm one of those people who reads the commentary in Jim's study Bible along with scripture, my eyes skip over more pages and I read, "Job's willingness to repent and confess known wrongs is a good guideline for us." Now, crybaby me is about to fall apart. This is what I need to do. I have to confess my sins and guilt over my baby. Why does it take half a lifetime to grow up or to make better decisions?

The night hours pass. I have no idea how long I ponder what my next step should be. I look at the clock on the wall. It's two-thirty in the morning. I close the Bible, turn out the light and start for the bedroom. I pause beside the music chest and instead of lifting the lid, I lay the Bible on top of it.

Tomorrow is going to come sooner than I imagine and Mr. Green and I will be working on presentations for the up-coming previews. I write a note on my pad of paper on the nightstand. "Remind self to ask Jim for his pastor's telephone number." I sleep soundly.

I want to throw my alarm clock across the room when it goes off at six o'clock, but I don't. I'm up, have my coffee and a piece of raisin toast. Just as I close my front door, I spot Mr. Green coming out of one of the stallion barns. He waves at me. I catch up to him.

"Is everything okay?" I put my hand over the top of my eyes to keep the morning sun at bay.

"Okay now. One of the stallions, our old Egyptian one, didn't feel so well this morning. Doc Means gave him the once over and we are going to keep an eye on him today. How was your trip? Oh, and I hope you don't mind, I weaseled your new job out of Jim."

"I sure hope it's nothing serious for the stallion! My trip was, well, interesting for sure. And, no I don't mind. I was going to tell you anyway." I poke his shoulder and grin. "It will never take the place of this job though, nothing can! It's just a hobby."

Mr. Green pokes me right back, smiling in relief!

I start to giggle and continue. "The extra money is welcome but I'm not so sure modeling is for me. I'm way more comfortable in my jeans, boots and having a horse to ride." We pass by the rose garden next to the office.

"My kind of girl!" Mr. Green gives me a high-five. He changes the subject. "Hey, look at these roses. Your dad is doing such a great job with them. You sure he's not a botanical engineer?" Once again, he taps the end of my nose.

Speaking of Dad, I see Aunt Mary's truck coming down the lane. She's bringing Dad back to the ranch. While I was away for the weekend, he stayed at her place. I'm so pleased. They have been good for each other.

Chapter Thirty-Nine

Another week passes quickly. It's already Sunday. Jim took Dad and me to Wiley Wranglers for dinner last night. I'm so pleased the Green family includes Dad in all of their lives. Dad and Aunt Mary seem to really enjoy one another's company too and I've found I don't have to be the one to keep Dad entertained.

Dad has also joined the Green's church and is becoming involved in the Men's League. He is often gone from the cottage more than I am. I marvel how well he's done since Mom's passing. I also wonder what's wrong with me, why I can't get on with my own life. I do have an appointment this afternoon with Pastor David at Jim's church. I dress quickly to get to the church on time.

I pull into the church's parking lot. Dad went to the early service with Aunt Mary and I pass them heading either home or maybe out to breakfast. I wave and press on the center of the steering column to toot my horn. They wave back. I also see Jim's truck parked by the church's entrance and Kent and Phyllis are pulling Jacob from his car seat. Great, maybe they won't see me and

I can find my favorite seat in the back. My meeting with Pastor David is a half hour after service ends.

I manage to wait in my car and watch the Green gang enter church before I get out and make my way to find a seat. Funny, when I step into an aisle, the same young woman who sat by me the last time I was here is in the same row. Not the one with the small baby. Anyway, she smiles at me when I scoot past her. I manage to tromp on her toes. "Oh, I'm sorry."

"No problem. There is hardly any room to pass and besides, I only need one or two toes to walk." She laughs, and then puts her hand out. "My name is Jenny. I think I sat by you once before." She bends her head slightly when she looks up at me.

"Yes, I believe we did sit next to each other. My name is Karen. Again, I'm so sorry." I sit down beside her and arrange my purse on the floor. Just before I start to say more to her, the praise team starts to sing. The song's first phrase is "Just breathe." Yes, I tell myself, breathe Karen, just breathe.

Once again, the pastor has had a hidden camera in my house! He talks about how we tend to make our prayers all about self. He reminds us that trust is all about understanding God knows our every need. He alone is in control. He encourages us to praise Him and seek His will. He says, "I pray we can go forward each day, live and walk in His footsteps, make a difference in someone else's life and be a beacon of light or testimony to bless another." I feel convicted once again. I do pray so much for my needs.

I scrunch down in my seat a little. 'Woe is me' certainly rolls off my lips every day. I'm so caught up in my thoughts I don't see the praise team has already finished the last song and Pastor David is dismissing the congregation. Jenny places her hand on mine.

"Karen, are you okay?" Lines bunch on her forehead. "You okay?"

"Yes, sorry. Guess I'm deep in thought. How do these pastors always seem to know my life is a mess?"

Jenny squeezes my hand. "I don't know, but they sure do, don't they?"

Her eyes are soft with concern. I must say something. "Thank you for your concern. Is this your home church?"

"Yes, I started coming over a year ago after my husband was killed in a skiing accident in Colorado. We used to vacation there every winter. I like the pastor but I'm not very involved here. How about you?"

Most of the people have filed out of the church. We continue to sit next to one another and a quiet settles around us.

"This is only my second time. I have an appointment to meet with Pastor David in thirty minutes. My husband also passed away. A car accident, shortly after we married."

It felt really weird to say the words out loud and to a stranger no less! I squirm in my seat.

"I'm so sorry. Do you live in Scottsdale? I live off Lone Mountain in a guest house in the back of a friend's property."

"Really? We are practically neighbors. I live in a cottage on the Green Ranch. Do you know them?"
Jenny's grin breaks into a wide smile. "That's crazy, my brother is one of the grooms at the ranch. Mr. Green gave my little girl one of his young horses. It has only one eye."

"Oh my gosh, Mr. Green told me about your daughter. I actually found the glass eye the first week I worked there. What a small world!" My shoulders relax and I settle back into my seat. I take a quick peek at my watch to make sure I'll be on time for my appointment with Pastor David.

"Here, let me give you my cell number. I'd love to get together with you sometime."

Jenny pushes herself up and grabs hold of me in a strong hug. "Oh, you can't know how that would please me. I'm also in need of a friend. Here, let me give you my number too."

We are like a couple of school kids. We plug each other's numbers into our phones, reach out and hug once again and Jenny actually skips out of the church just as Pastor David walks through the entrance toward me.

Chapter Forty

Pastor David and I start off a little cautious with one another. We introduce ourselves and he asks if he can sit next to me. I scoot over to give him ample room. My hand trembles when I grasp his with a firm handshake. Like many men often do when I shake hands, he scowls.

"Now that's a handshake. Let me see if I still have my fingers." He sits back and laughs. "So, tell me Karen, how can I help you? I do know you are the young lady Mr. Green hired and I also know you have suffered a few trials in a very short time."

Pastor David must see my eyebrows shoot upward. He reaches a hand toward me. "Mr. Green shared only this much with me Karen, nothing more. He hoped you might start coming to services and only told me, so I could more or less reach out to you, if you did. We are a big family here. I try to be available to our family members with their needs. So, let me start again. I'm here to listen, not judge, only our Lord judges."

I feel at ease. Pastor David seems genuine. I like him immediately. A sigh escapes my lips and old cry baby me lets my tears fall. "I don't know where to begin. I'm such a mess. I don't understand why God let my husband, and now, my mother die. I don't know where to place my grief. Some days are better than others, but I can't stop feeling furious at God for my loss. When people are hurting this way, they often ask God "why?""

Pastor David leans back into his seat. He swipes his hand across his forehead and releases a whooshing sound from deep within his chest. "Boy, Karen, isn't that the million-dollar question?" He folds his arms across his chest.

"I wish I could come up with answers to help bring you to complete peace about your losses. I just know most of us cannot postpone or even control when we might die. I think it is really hard to push aside the why question and get on with… what can I do about it now that it's happened."

My shoulders start to relax as I listen to Pastor David's words. He smiles at me and continues.

"Karen, I don't believe God always sends us the trial but I do believe He gives us strength to deal with it. I also know many of us question the why of plane crashes, tornadoes, floods and other disasters, but these are natural disasters. Harold Kushner says in his book, "When Bad Things Happen To Good People," that "Nature is blind, without values." He says, "God stands for justice, for fairness, for compassion."

Pastor David shifts in his seat when he looks at me and sees more tears fall freely from my eyes.

"I don't know if I'm making you feel better or worse Karen." He leans forward. "Hey, I keep a copy of Kushner's book in my office. I really think it could be beneficial for you to read. Should I go get it?" He tilts his head to the side and raises one eyebrow.

I can hardly answer him, so I shake my head up and down and pull tissues from my purse. While I wait for him to return, I think about how and what I can do about my grief. It simply is what it is. I've heard about Kushner's book. I hope it might help. I also know I must tell Pastor David about my baby and my guilt. I'm just not sure I can today.

Chapter Forty-One

I leave church with the book tucked under my arm. As I'm coming down the lane into the ranch, my mood softens. Just look, the babies are running with such freedom in the open fields. Most of them have been weaned from their mothers. They are becoming independent teens searching for their spot and purpose on this earth. Maybe it's about time for me to search for some purpose and quit thinking about myself. I laugh out loud when I spot Jim waving his arms from the breeding barn.

When I get close enough, I see a look of panic on Jim's face. I drive close as possible to the barn, park the car and jump out. "What's wrong Jim?"

Jim grabs my arm and drags me into one of the stalls where I see Doc Grady on his hands and knees attempting to help one of our late bred mares deliver her foal. Jim and I press our faces to the bars of the stall.

Jim begins to fill me in. "This is Shasta. She is not due for some time and the foal will most likely die."

Because I just came from my meeting with Pastor David, this is not what I need to witness. Die, why? I hesitate, and then I surprise myself when I pull the stall door open and put my hand on Doc Grady's back. "What can I do? How can I help?"

Doc looks at me and shakes his head side to side. Just then the tiny filly is released from the mare's womb. Doc starts to clear away the embryonic sac and the filly takes in a large breath and begins to wiggle. At the same time, Jim is now in the stall cradling the mare's head. He looks at me and mouths the words. "She's gone."

The filly continues to wiggle and show signs that she is a fighter. Even though it isn't winter and cold, Doc Grady takes off his shirt and asks me to get a blanket. I move faster than I think possible and come back with several blankets, which he wraps the filly in. I take note that the filly's hooves haven't completely formed yet. How can she live, I wonder. I try to shake off the dread about to swallow me. I begin to compare this preemie filly with the loss of my child. Not realistic, sure, but it hits me hard for reasons I can't understand. I think I need to make another appointment with Pastor David.

The rest of the day passes with a flurry of activity to help the new filly. The entire ranch is on call to be available for duty. Doc Grady decides to stay in the stall with the filly until he is sure everything will go smoothly, since there are so many supplements and medicines he will need to administer. I'm in awe over the commitment and loyalty he has for actually living in a stall for who knows how long!

Jim rides back toward the cottage with me so I can drop him off at the main house on my way. "Thanks, Karen for being there with us. Doc says he really believes in miracles and this might be one."

I reach across the front seat to touch Jim's hand. "No, Jim, let me thank you. I have never felt so wanted. I want so much to do whatever I can to help any of you. Thank you for always being there for me. I'm a big pain in the neck sometimes and the Green family just takes me in stride. I love all of you for this."

Jim places his hand across my cheek. "Oh Karen, you have no idea how you bless my family. Please don't forget, I will continue to be very patient." He brings my fingers to his mouth and kisses them sweetly. "How about dinner tonight? Maybe the old diner on Fifth Avenue?"

"Yes, Jim. Pick me up about six." I drive away with two thoughts boring into my brain. I must talk to Pastor David and I think I'm fooling myself because I believe I do enjoy the attention Jim gives me and I really care for him.

Chapter Forty-Two

I can't believe the summer has nearly disappeared. How can it possibly be October already? So much has happened. I stretch my arms above my head this morning before I need to be dressed and out the door to present another Sunday preview. The smile I feel spread across my face is indicative of all the good things I've accomplished already this summer.

I finally had my talk with Pastor David. He was so gentle and kind with his words when I poured my heart out to him. I confessed my desire to abort my baby by riding Ibn as fast and as hard as I could through the desert hills. I told him how my anger at God has nearly destroyed me to be good to anyone else. I even shared that I have feelings for Jim and don't know how to let him know. I also asked Pastor David if he thought I was being unfaithful to Jess. The conversation went something like this:

Pastor David said, "So Karen, you tell me that before you married Jess, you met with a pastor, said a profession of faith after a confession. Do you feel like your life changed? Have you continued to read your

Bible and strengthen your relationship with Christ?"

"Can I be honest?" I ask. "But of course I can," I mumble to myself. "When Jess and I married, I couldn't put the Bible down. It overwhelmed me to see how the Bible is such a guidebook. Then after the accident I blamed God for everything. I realize now what a selfish, self-centered person I've become and... no, I don't read my Bible anymore. I don't even know if I understand what it means to have Jesus living in me."

Pastor David moved to his desk and picked up his Bible. "I appreciate your honesty Karen. When we confess our sins and believe in our hearts that God raised Jesus from the grave and he died for our sins, the term we use is, we've been born again."

I interrupted, "Yes, I understand all of this, but just what really makes us different than another person who is not a believer?" I leaned forward anxious to hear his answer.

He said, "I think what makes us different, Karen, are the God like qualities in our lives. If we sincerely want Christ in our hearts, then we need to really get to know God by reading our Bibles daily. I believe this is the only way we can understand what He asks of us as believers. I'm not saying we can ever be sin free like Christ, but our lives need to conform to what we are asked to believe." Pastor David leaned across his desk and took my hands in his.

"We should be full of God's love and actively show love to others. We cannot judge others in our lives. After talking to so many people, I think the hardest thing to do is to trust God with our lives during hardships or temptations. What you are struggling with, Karen is so common. I believe all Christians have to work hard to remain faithful. I think we all fail."

Pastor David smiles and shrugs his shoulders. "I have to work just as hard as the next person. I know for sure, though, God forgives our failures as long as we recognize them, confess and move on to follow in His footsteps as best we can. I believe the most important thing which makes us different is, scripture tells us, we will live forever in heaven with our Savior." Pastor David patted the top of his closed Bible. He released a deep sigh.

"You have professed your faith, Karen. You can offer your confessions to Him. God loves you and His holy spirit will carry you through many trials in your life if you will surrender your fears and put your life at His feet."

This is when I fell to my knees and begged for forgiveness. Words tumbled out of my mouth. I said, "Please God, forgive me for wanting to take the life of my unborn child through abortion and then in being so reckless with its care to the point which I may even have caused its miscarriage. I pray it was Thy will rather than my own doing, but if it was my fault then please, please forgive me. Forgive me also for not trusting your will for my family and me. I'm so sorry for all the wrongs in my life." I asked for forgiveness for all the months I doubted God's word and His love for me. Pastor David lifted me gently from the floor and let me cry on his shoulder. I walked away from church that morning and felt at peace.

***

I know Pastor David is right about everything he said. I feel ashamed I let so many months go by with so much anger in my heart. I know everything he said is true and if Jess were here, he would have recited the very same speech to me.

Now, this morning I kick the pebbles out of my way with a renewed feeling of hope and I'm ready to give the very best preview I can put together. My heart feels open and free.

I smell the coffee brewing in the kitchen. Dad must be up. I dress quickly and head toward the strong aroma.

"Morning, Daddy."

"Good morning, Angel, I poured your coffee. I'm up early this morning because Mary and I are going to Payson to picnic. We thought it would be good to get out of the heat for the afternoon. We may stay the night, so if I don't get home…not to worry."

I think I see his eyes twinkle. I sit down, wrap my fingers around my coffee cup and tilt my head. "Is there something you need to tell me?"

Dad sits across from me and points his cup in my direction. "Just what is it you'd like to hear?" He sips his coffee, all the while his eyes stare into mine, and he says, "I think you are curious as to what my intentions are toward your Aunt Mary." He sets his cup down and reaches out to take both my hands in his. "I really enjoy Mary, Karen, and I believe she feels the same about me. We spend a lot of time together, as you know. We may, in the near future, decide we want to spend the rest of our lives together. Does this answer your question?"

I grip his hands tight. I'm not sure what I feel.

Dad gets up and pulls me into his arms. "It doesn't mean Karen, I don't still love your mother or I don't think of her every day. I will always love her."

Dad pushes me an arm's length away. Tears make their way down his cheeks.

"Mary has been alone over five years now and we have so much in common and we make each other laugh. I think we will be good for one another. I hope you approve?"

I feel like my heart is going to burst with joy. "Oh Daddy, I'm so thrilled for you. How can I not approve of Aunt Mary? She is amazing. And Daddy… Mom surely approves. Way to keep all the love within the family tree." We embrace again and laugh until our stomachs hurt.

Chapter Forty-Three

The arena is prepared. The trainers are decked out in just the right flare of red, white and blue. A red and blue bolo type tie clutches the neck of their starched white shirts and their black riding pants and black boots put the final touches on Mr. Green's requirements.

The stands fill up fast. I check my mike at the podium in the middle of the arena. Then I give a nod to the groom who handles the PA system. The barn staff spends hours grooming the sale horses. A special crew spruces the six stallions days ahead of time. The horses' coats gleam like waxed cars. Their long tails and manes glisten after much brushing and conditioning. Preview morning, the stallions' manes are dressed with roses. The roses are placed over their heads just like the tradition at a Kentucky Derby presentation. A groom places special wraps on the lower part of the horses' legs to prevent them from nicking themselves during a run in the arena.

Mr. Green sits off to the side of the stands in his golf cart. He gives me a signal.

"Good morning ladies and gentlemen. Welcome. Would you all please stand for our National Anthem?"

Immediately, the arena gate opens and one of our trainers rides into the arena on our Egyptian stallion. Secured to the saddle on the right side of the horse, a flagpole with a flag waves in the morning breeze. It brings the crowd to their feet. The intercom blares and the crowd breaks out in a chorus of united voice. The applause reaches a deafening pitch when the stallion takes a deep bow and our rider speeds around the arena and out the gate.

I give a little history on the Arabian horse. I speak about pedigree and encourage the crowd to cheer, clap and whistle. Upbeat music plays on a loud speaker. Noise from the crowd actually encourages magnificent performances from each horse.

I've been doing these previews for four weeks now and every preview I repeat a story about one particular horse. Those who came the Sundays before sometimes blurt my favorite saying out loud, along with me. We preview a mare by the name of Miss Diamond. I always ask the ladies in the audience; "Now ladies, would you rather have a diamond on your finger or this diamond in your backyard?" Enter...Miss Diamond. She prances into the arena with huge front leg action, reaching up and forward. More deafening noise rises from the crowd. The women scream the loudest!

To my surprise, the trainer doesn't release the mare. She guides the horse straight toward me. I worry the mare might be hurt or sick. The trainer moves in closer to the podium before she asks me for the microphone.

Confused, I hand it to her. She takes it and says. "Karen, your boss is sick and tired of hearing you talk about having a diamond in your backyard. For this reason, he has decided to give Miss Diamond to you. Now you can feed her!" The crowd goes wild. Mr. Green smiles at me from the golf cart. Deeply touched, I put my hand over my heart. Our eyes meet and he raises his hand and waves at me. Miss Diamond is released. She proves her worth as a prized Bask daughter when she puts on a show of elegance.

I'm stunned. As the crowd continues to scream, I hold my tears at bay. Of course, I don't have a tissue. When I look over my shoulder, I see Jim approach with a box of them. I guess he really does know me well, He knows my dry eyes won't last!

I find a way to compose myself and the rest of the preview goes off without a flaw. The crowd starts to disperse. Most of the people take time to go through the barns and see the horses we just previewed. Others tour the entire ranch by taking rides in a carriage pulled by four of Mr. Green's miniature horses.

Jim waits for me when I turn to step down from my podium. He looks like a little boy with some sort of secret. His hat is pushed back on his head so that it frames his ears. I want to laugh. Instead I say.

"Did you know your dad was going to give me Miss Diamond?" I take his hand and move from the last step. "I'm shocked and thrilled at the same time."

"I didn't know when he was going to do it, but he shared his secret with the family last night. Oh, and did you know that she is carrying your future ride?"

He laughs and pulls me in to his chest with his best bear hug.

Now, my tears fall freely down my cheeks. "Really?" I return his hug and I suddenly realize that I don't want to let go of him. I whisper in his ear. "I must be the luckiest girl alive." I squeeze my eyes closed and think to myself the pebbles in my shoes may be a thing of the past.

Chapter Forty-Four

After a very full weekend, Dad's news, a preview with surprises, I actually look forward to Monday. Daddy didn't get home last night, so I assume he and Aunt Mary are having a wonderful time. My coffee is getting cold because I'm daydreaming about the past few days. I get up from the kitchen table and pass by the living room window. The shutter is open a few inches and I think I see balloons. What…

I open the shutters completely. Tied to the white picket fence at the end of the lane to my cottage, I see at least ten yellow balloons. The sprinkler has come on and the balloons seem to dance as the drops of water hit them.

I run out the front door, still in my robe. I see each balloon has writing on it. The sprinkler is still going as I duck my head and pull at the strings attached to the post. I'm laughing so hard by the time I get back to the doorway of the cottage I fall through the entrance into the living room.

I still have the strings in my hand while I lie on my back. With the strings in my left hand, I use my right hand to pull one balloon at a time down to eye level and start to read. One by one, I release a balloon. Every one of them says the same thing. "Karen Anderson, will you marry me?"

Talk about shock waves surging through a body. I lie here on the floor for what feels like hours before I feel like I can get to my feet. I'm somewhat numb. I roll over and push myself to an upright position and feel my body sway. I make my way to the bathroom and stare at myself in the mirror.

It takes me longer to get ready for my day because, for obvious reasons, my head reels. The ranch seems unusually quiet as I make my way to the office. However, when I get to my desk, I see that everything is operating just like any other day. Lois is busy with Mr. Green in his office, probably taking some shorthand because I can hear Mr. Green's confident voice giving her some instructions.

The accountant is hammering away at his adding machine and I have a stack of pedigrees on the edge of my desk which need changes made to them. The only odd thing I notice is my calendar sits on the middle of my desk. I reach down to move it and see someone has circled today, Monday, with a red marker. Alongside the day, I read, "Today, I want you to know ... my patience has run out. Pick you up for dinner at seven."

I don't know whether to cry or laugh. Instead, I tell myself to take a deep breath. I get up and march directly into Mr. Green's office. "Excuse me Mr. Green and Lois. I'm going down to the stallion barn. I just wanted to let you know in case the phone rings, I won't be here to answer it. I should return shortly."

I don't give either of them time to answer before I nearly run out of the office and toward the stallion barn. I throw my shoulders back and let my now long curls blow in the breeze. I don't even know who I am. I feel my mouth widen into a gaping hole while laughter fills the air.

Just as I turn into the stallion barn, I come face to face with Jim. I throw my arms around his neck and we fall into a heap right there in front of at least four stall cleaners and several grooms. "Yes, Jim, I will marry you." I look in those blue eyes and say. "But not until I get to know you much better, like maybe a year from now."

Jim picks himself up and reaches an outstretched hand to pull me off the ground. By this time everyone standing by is applauding and hollering. "Whoop, whoop hooray!" Jim picks up his hat and waves it in front of his waist.

"Well, Miss Karen, I think those terms are quite alright with me." Then he pulls me into his arms and plants a kiss on my lips.

He turns, grabs hold of me in a fireman lift and carries me all the way back to the office while I squeal like a little girl.

We burst through the office door with such clatter that Mr. Green and Lois run out to see what's going on. Jim tips his hat as he speaks first, "Daddy, Karen and I are engaged. We aren't getting married right away, you understand, after about a year but we wanted you to be the first to know, we will be married!"

Jim puts me down next to him. I know my face must be crimson red. Can this be happening? Before I can question anything else, Mr. Green picks me up in his arms and swings me in circles. Lois starts to cry and holds her hands together in prayer position while looking to the ceiling.

My head spins. Mr. Green puts me down. "This calls for a celebration. Tonight, dinner is on me. Lois, make all the arrangements, call the kids, get ahold of Paul and Mary and make reservations at The Mansion Restaurant at eight. You come too, Lois!"

He puts his fingers under my chin. "You, my pretty one, take the day off." He turns toward Jim. "And you, my handsome son, you need to spend it with her. I'll expect you both at dinner. No hanky panky...you hear?"

Jim salutes his father, gently puts his hand in mine and turns me toward the front door.

Chapter Forty-Five

Something starts to change in me. I begin to pray more about my blessings at night. My prayers start to include more understanding that I'm not in control. I also start to see prayers answered because I think less of wants, my desires and myself. I start to really believe my gifts and skills dealing with clients and life in general are from God. I have no way of explaining this to anyone. I just feel it.

So, as I sit here this morning with my hot cup of coffee, I watch a mother bird feed her baby who peeks out of their nest in the branches of a large Cottonwood tree by my kitchen window. The winter has zoomed by. It seems like yesterday when Jim proposed to me. I recount some of the special moments these past months.

***

Jim and I had spent the whole day together after he proposed. We rode north in his truck and spent the afternoon in Oak Creek Canyon. We sat beside the creek and skipped stones across the water. We talked about our pasts, our mistakes, our dreams and our future together.

We brought up the upcoming anniversary of my accident. Jim spoke softly when he shared how he felt when the anniversary of his girlfriend's passing came around. He told me to take all the time I needed to process my grief.

I was completely honest. I explained how I felt a little guilty when I realized I had feelings for him. I felt like I betrayed my love for Jess. Jim shared his feelings, which were much the same, but how he felt confident Stacy would want him to find love again and be happy. Of course, Jess had told me many times, that if anything ever happened to him he wanted me to find love again.

The next few months Jim and I dated like teenagers. Dinners, movies, sunrise and sunset trail rides and hikes along the edges of Camelback Mountain once it cooled off were things we loved to do. It felt so good to laugh again.

The previews, on Sundays, gave Jim and me reason to attend church together on Saturday nights. We also became involved in the growth group on Thursday evenings. This was a group of single people our age who were recovering from divorce or a loss of a spouse or friend. All forms of loss are difficult. The group spoke out boldly and the conversations were sincere and helpful. Support offered from everyone was genuine and full of love. I grew a lot in my faith during this time.

And... my daddy and Mary... well, they too were getting to know one another. Daddy comes home every night to the cottage, still attends to Mr. Green's roses and helps around the ranch, but he spends most of his late afternoons and evenings with Mary. He has even convinced Mary to get back on a horse and they ride the mountain trails like a couple of kids. I wonder how long it will be before they get hitched. I'm sure my mom smiles down at them.

Sylvia kept calling through the winter to ask me to audition for various modeling stints. I did a few of them so I could stash the money in a savings account. But, for the most part I turned her offers down. I was much busier at the ranch during the winter season with all the sales we ran and the major Scottsdale All Arabian Show our trainers and ranch staff were involved in during the month of February.

Debee and Bill had a beautiful little girl, who they named Julie. I don't hear from her as much as before, after all she is a mommy now and her focus is on mothering. She keeps telling me when little Julie gets older they will make a road trip and come see us. She and Bill were super excited to hear about Jim. We'll see...

Jenny and I have become good friends and she attends the growth group with me and Jim. She is dating a wonderful man from our church. Her little girl will begin showing her horse in a few years and still keeps busy after school at the ranch. She can't wait to plaster winner's ribbons all over the walls in her room. Now that's a positive attitude!

And believe it or not, the filly who was born too early actually lived. Our vet never thought it was possible. Another mare who had lost her foal a few weeks earlier accepted the filly and she is doing well.

***

Wow, so much has happened. The red wild poppies are already in bloom, most of the mares have foaled and I can hardly believe Jim continues to be so patient about me deciding on a wedding date. I move from the kitchen with a fresh cup of coffee and settle in my favorite rocking chair. I pick up my Bible. I read, "For I know the plans I have for you, declares the Lord. They are plans to prosper you and not harm you. Plans to give you hope and a future."
I love this verse, but sometimes it's still hard for me to trust God knows what's best for

me. I see for myself the amazing changes taking place in my life since I surrendered myself into His hands last year. I do see hope for my future and I do realize I will have trials and sadness in my life. I know I still fall from His grace and have to repent often. Dang, it's a constant work in progress to try to walk in His footsteps.

I look down at my beautiful rich brown colored leather bound study Bible. Jim bought it for me this past Christmas. I've tucked Jess's Bible safely into his music chest. I've also made pillows out of Jess's robe. I know, I know, you must be laughing. I saw a pattern on Pinterest, the world's catalog of ideas, and snip, snip, three soft cuddly pillows evolved which I throw on the bed. I actually washed the robe until I couldn't smell Jess's aftershave any longer. It just seemed like the right thing to do.

Chapter Forty-Six

My thoughts are interrupted because my phone rings. I smile when I see Jim's picture pop up on the screen. I love his grin. He looks like he is about to spill the world's most sacred secret. "Good morning, I was just thinking about you."

"And obviously, I was just thinking about you because I called you." He laughs. "I thought we might take a ride up by McDowell Mountain this morning. I can load the horses in the trailer and be by to pick you up in half an hour. Last week the wild horses were at the bottom of the mountain and I spotted a few foals. I've already packed a lunch."

"Well, Mr. have it all together, how can I resist such an offer? I just need to take a quick shower and dress. I'll be ready."

This is something else I love about Jim. He can be so spontaneous. We haven't been on a ride on a Saturday in at least a month. I shower, dress and wait by the end of my walkway with my thumb in the air when he arrives. I notice there are two bay horses in the trailer. "Hey, who did you bring? I don't see Ibn?"

Jim jumps out of the truck and springs toward the passenger side to open the door for me. "I brought Aza Dazzle because she's looking a little plump and she needs some exercise. Hope you don't mind?"

"No, no not at all. I love her spirit and yes she does look a little plump." I reach over and plant a quick kiss on Jim's cheek. "Thanks for being so concerned about we women and our weight." I feign a wide-eyed 'whatever' type look.

Jim punches playfully at my shoulder. We sit back and enjoy each other's company. I love that we are so comfortable together. And of course, he turns on the CD player and pops in good 'ole Stevie Wonder. We belt out, "I Just Called To Say I Love You" in our best vocals.

Once we have the horses out of the trailer, Jim walks toward me and gives me one of his bear hugs. "I love you Karen Anderson. Is that marriage date getting any closer?"

I'm still in his arms when I tap him on the nose with a finger. "Funny you should ask Mr. Green. I marked August 28 on my calendar just this morning." I feel a chuckle groaning to get out of my throat but I remain serious.

Jim starts to shout at the top of his lungs, "Yes, yes, thank you Lord." He picks me up and swings me in circles. Both horses shy. His horse, Jake, lets out a noisy whinny and stomps his hooves. Jim cradles my face in his hands. "Thank you Karen, you have made me the happiest man in the world."

"And you, Jim, have made me want to live again." I brush my lips across his and turn toward the horses. "We're burning daylight!"

The McDowell Mountains are already lush with wild spring flowers. Some of the cacti, especially the prickly pear are budded but not quite open.

We've ridden about half an hour, when Jim spots the wild herd. "Karen, look to your left."

A herd of about fifteen are grazing on some of the brush grass. Most of them are bay color. Hidden under a mesquite tree I see a lighter Palomino with a foal by her side. Her foal has a perfect white shaped heart on her hip. I point to her. "Look, Jim, love is everywhere!" The wet sparkle in his blue eyes sends chills down my back. He nods.

We ride for several hours. When we return to the truck, I water the horses and hang hay bags on the side of the trailer for them. Jim is already spreading a blanket and all the goodies from the picnic basket he brought. I'm certain Phyllis must have fried the chicken and made the potato salad and the cherry pie looks like her work as well.

She and Kent are so excited about our impending marriage.

Jim has even brought a bottle of wine. He pops the cork and hands me a glass for a toast. "Here's to August 28 and our happily ever after."

I bump his glass. "To our happily ever after."

The sun is beginning to set just as we pack the truck, put the horses in the trailer and head for home.

We drive down the lane and turn toward my cottage. I notice some activity in the barn next to my place. It isn't unusual to see our vet's truck any given day on the farm so I don't give it much thought. Jim reaches across the seat and takes my hand. I turn to look at him and the look I see in his eyes frightens me. "Jim? What's wrong?"

He squeezes my fingers. "It might be Ibn, Karen. This morning he wasn't doing well. I'm so sorry I didn't tell you but I thought I needed to get you away for the day. Dad promised me he would call me if it looked serious. Please don't be mad."

I'm out of the truck and running. My heart beats so hard in my chest, I can hardly breathe. The sliding doors on the barn are already open. I trip over my own feet and fall onto Mr. Green.

"Whoa there, girl." Mr. Green steadies me. "He is okay for now. We are just watching him. Karen, look at me." Mr. Green plants both hands on my shoulders. "Ibn is twenty-seven Karen. He has given us many great years. We may need to let him go."

I'm trying to listen to his voice, but my mind yells no, no! My body slips from Mr. Green's hold. I sit on the barn floor and sob. I've lost dogs and cats in my lifetime, but never an animal like Ibn. I feel I'm about to lose a real part of myself. It's the same feeling I had when Jess died. I know that sounds stupid to some people. "It's only an animal," I've heard people say so often.

Jim sits next to me, his arms folded around me. "I understand Karen. He has been such a part of your life when you were a teen and now, this past year, such solace for you when you needed it." Jim's fingers sweep my bangs from my face. "Let's go in the stall and sit with him. Okay?"

The vet moves from the stall door when we come forward. Ibn is lying down and Aunt Mary is in the stall. Ibn's head is propped in her lap. Her tears fall freely down her face. She looks up at me and pats a space in the shavings next to her. Jim helps me sit down and I lean against Aunt Mary's shoulder. Ibn's eyes are open and if it's possible to see pain in horse's eyes, I'm sure I see it.

"Aunt Mary, what are we going to do?" I know what her answer is going to be but I don't want to hear it. I cover my ears with my hands and shake my head back and forth. "I know, I know." I cry harder.

Aunt Mary raises my chin. "We can't let him suffer Karen. His kidneys have failed. He's in pain." She tells our Vet, "It's time."

I throw myself across Ibn's chest and stroke his neck. "Goodbye sweet friend."

Jim pulls me away and lifts me up and into his arms. He holds me tighter than I've ever felt before and I need his strength right now. Aunt Mary stands and throws her arms around both of us. In a tight circle, we mourn.

The evening doesn't seem to want to end. We all come back to the main house. Phyllis and Kent put a bountiful dinner on the table. We speak in soft voices.

Occasionally someone laughs, obvious to all, an effort to lighten our moods. Jim is more than attentive to my needs. He is quick to remind us. "I'm so grateful for all the joy Ibn brought to so many."

Aunt Mary says, "Not only all the joy he gave to my family, let's not forget the developmentally challenged adults who used to come from the ARC of Arizona to ride him. His gentle spirit brought giggles of joy to these special people."

"You're both right: Jim and Aunt Mary." I glance at Aunt Mary, who sits next to my daddy. I know they hold hands under the table. "Aunt Mary, I'm so sorry. I know how hard this must be for you."

Aunt Mary lowers her head. Remnants of tears stain her face. "Yes, it is hard. I remember all the years when Joe trained Ibn. He used to come in the house and rave about how smart he was. He used to tell me, "That dang horse is almost human. I swear he understands everything I ask of him."

Now our conversation starts to sound almost raucous as we all vie for stories to share, hoping to bring back memories to make us laugh and cry. I begin to see the blessing in all of this. God gave us twenty-seven years of this amazing animal. Not many horses live so long. Look at this table. A gathering of family, united to support one another. Yep, God is good.

Chapter Forty-Seven

Wedding day is upon us. We decide to have the ceremony in the middle of the sales barn. It's still pretty warm since it's late August, but the sales barn is air-conditioned. Aunt Mary and Phyllis go all out on decorations.

Blankets of yellow roses line the barn ceiling. They bribed all the grooms and stall workers to push each rose stem into a mesh veil they attached to the ceiling. We decided to leave the sale horses in their stalls. Each horse is groomed and manes and tails are trussed in yellow roses as well. Stall doors are draped with curled yellow ribbons and one single yellow rose with a sprig of Baby's Breath.

I'm in the cottage sitting in the rocking chair Jess gave me. I pull his Bible from the top of the music chest and it sits on my lap. My hands rub over the cover and I can almost hear his voice, "All is good, Karen. This is just what I want for you. I know you will never forget me." I close my eyes. I pull his Bible to my chest. I hear a soft knock at the door.

"It's me, Karen, Daddy. Can I come in? I know you will be getting dressed soon, but I just wanted to have a few minutes with you."

I get up so quick I drop the Bible on the floor in front of me. "Oh, Daddy, yes come in."

I'm in his arms and all I hear him say is, "Mom would be so happy for you. Jess is so happy for you, I know this, Karen."

I push Dad an arm's length away. "I know too, Daddy. Sometimes I can't believe this is happening to me. I'm certainly not a kid anymore and I'm really sad it has taken me so long to let go and trust God. Two marriages down and God gives me yet another chance for happiness. Remember how I've told you I've felt my whole life has been like I lived it with pebbles in my shoe?" Dad's eyebrows rise when he looks intently into my eyes.

"Well, I'm beginning to feel less of that feeling." I fall into his arms. Time seems to stand still before there is another knock at the door.

"It's me, Aunt Mary. Time for the bride to get dressed." She walks toward us. We group hug. "Okay, Paul, time for you to get out. We girls have to get ready." She playfully pushes him toward the door.

Dad salutes Aunt Mary. "Aye, aye captain." Then with a bow to the waist he says, "Do you think she will be so bossy when we get married?" He laughs all the way to the golf cart he drove to the cottage.

"Really, Aunt Mary? Are you... really?" I watch a crimson red creep up her neck and spill throughout her face.

I grab her hands. We dance in a circle. "Come on girl, we need to get you dressed." Aunt Mary drags me toward the bedroom. My very pale yellow dress is draped over the bed. I slip it over my head. Aunt Mary secures the long line of tiny pearl buttons down the back of my gown.

"I thought you might want to wear these? They were your mothers." She turns me to look into the floor length mirror. She places a string of pearls around my neck. Tiny yellow roses peek out between each pearl.

"Oh, how perfect, Aunt Mary. You're going to make me cry. Good thing I haven't done my makeup yet." We hug, then giggle like teenagers. I finish putting on my makeup and sit down to put on my pale-yellow boots. Even my boots have pearl studs scattered around the top of the toes.

I chose yellow roses for the theme of my wedding because yellow was my mother's favorite color and her favorite flower was the rose. The color yellow is also a cheerful symbol of renewal and when yellow daisies bloom, they seem to bloom forever, even when I cut them and put them in a vase. Yellow, for me, is a happy color.

I'm amazed how calm I feel when Aunt Mary and I get in the golf cart parked in front of the cottage. The staff has decorated the cart to match everything in the barn. I feel a little like a princess in my unique carriage as we bump along over the road to make our way to the sale barn.

I see some of the family walking to the barn. Phyllis has hold of Jacobs's hand. He has a dark blue suit on and matching tie. Jacob hurries ahead of Phyllis, pulling her arm with all his might. He will carry the rings. I feel an old pang of guilt. Will it ever go away?

We drive the cart off to one side of the main barn and wait for a cue for my entrance. Jenny's brother is going to play Stevie Wonder's song, our song, Jim's and mine. Now, I start to feel some butterflies churning in my stomach. I hear the first few notes.

Aunt Mary slips into the barn and I stand here by myself. I walk slowly toward the open doors of the barn. I can't believe how beautiful everything looks. My heart melts when I catch sight of Jim. He stands by his father who has placed one hand on Jim's shoulder. I had no idea Jim was going to wear a pale-yellow suit to match my dress. I feel giddy and light headed. Daddy steps next to me and tucks my hand around his forearm. He steadies me. "Ready?"

"Yes, Daddy, very ready."

"Let's do this girl."

He walks me down the aisle and toward Jim where Jim takes my hand. I think I'm going to sink through the wood shavings on the ground. Pastor David's smile stretches to the corners of his eyes. Dad kisses my cheek and joins the rest of the family and the Green staff.

"I do's" are said, cheers break out, and the newly wed Mr. and Mrs. Green walk out the barn doors through a spray of Skittles candies, just as before with Jess; this time only the yellow colored ones! It must have taken the staff hours to sift through bags of Skittles and pull out just the yellow ones just to stay with the yellow theme!

Chapter Forty-Eight

I can't believe this fairy tale I'm living. I've moved into Jim's house and Daddy is living in the cottage by himself. He and Aunt Mary are talking about a possible Christmas wedding. I get all giddy just thinking about Daddy finding happiness again with Mom's sister. How crazy is this turn of events?

Jim and I settled into married life like the fit of an old pair of tennis shoes. Every day I wake up in his arms and feel such wonderment. How can it be possible I'd feel this happy again? I've finally lost the feeling I betrayed Jess, mainly because Jim lets me talk openly about my life with Jess. We don't hold any secrets from one another. He once said to me, "You have to be you and I have to be me, that's the only way we can be us." I had him repeat it several times.

And, so, I can be as silly as I often am. I can cry over the least little thing. I can take on a modeling gig if I want to, and I can pull out my pad of paper and journal to my heart's content. Jim can smoke a pipe in the garden area of our small fenced back yard; He can run in the mornings with Trouble or take him hunting on weekends during Elk season... even though I can't imagine shooting an Elk... once it is beautifully cooked though, I admit I love the flavor. Finally, and most importantly, we can worship together in the privacy of our home and join our church family for spiritual nurturing and fellowship. Yes, life is good ... the pebbles have disappeared.

***

Work never feels like work. I love waking to the sounds of horses whinnying. Jim always has the coffee made, we share breakfast and I'm off to the office and he heads toward the barns. We seldom see each other during the daytime hours unless I'm taking pictures of the horses, then Jim is usually a part of staging where we set up.

This morning I have an appointment for a regular checkup with my GYN. I hate these appointments; but after all, I am a woman and it's just part of our makeup to have yearly doctor visits. Jim and I have been married almost eight months. Since I am forty-four now, I feel it's even more important to have checkups. I have a dear friend who found out she has uterine cancer and she's only fifty. Always good to just make sure nothing is going on. Anyway, my appointment is at nine, so I'll go there first before work.

I arrive twenty minutes early. My fingers leaf through the typical array of dated magazines ... doesn't anyone ever think of updating them? I spy a stack of pamphlets on one of the side tables. A bright pink colored one sits on top. Big bold letters read: Women and Menopause. I start to flip through the pages. All the while my eyes scan the information, I think, yep, maybe this is what I must be going through. The depressing information lists symptoms. You know, hot flashes, mood swings, hair loss and worst of all, weight gain. I check off every item on the list in my head.

A nurse taps a pen on her clipboard. She interrupts my morose thoughts. "Mrs. Green, the doctor is ready for you." She ushers me to an examination room. She hands me one of those dang white gowns adorned with tiny blue polka dots. Before she walks out of the room, she asks me to undress, put the gown on and tie it in front. It seems like only seconds before she walks back in and waves a hand toward the exam table where she wants me to sit.

I position myself on thin white paper that stretches lengthwise across the table. I've mentioned before how the skimpy paper rips every time I change positions. Yep, there it goes! The nurse places my feet in wiggly stirrups attached to the table. A smile widens on her face showing her perfect straight white teeth. She says, "The doctor will be in shortly."

Or in an hour, I say to myself. My lips come together to hum softly to music, which filters in the room through an intercom. I tap my fingers on the side of the table to the beat of a Country Western song I don't recognize.

Doctor Anderson's jolly "hello" brings me back to the reality of the exam. I pull the light blanket the nurse gave me closer to my waist.

I feel my shoulders tense when she sits on a little stool at the foot of the table to prepare for the exam. I lift my eyes to the ceiling to avoid looking at her mouth, which appears to be frozen in a grin. Suddenly, she stops. Through my parted knees I watch her brows pull together. Wrinkles bunch up in squiggly lines across her forehead. She says, "Karen, do you know that you are about three months pregnant?"

I almost stand upright in the stirrups. I yelp when my right toe catches the edge of the stirrup. A hand pops up in a limp gesture to wave at her while the other hand forces my dropped jaw back into place. Then I laugh out loud. "Oh, that's real funny." When I spit out the words, I don't recognize my own strangled voice. Is the bile I feel creep from my throat and threaten to come to the back of my teeth there because I'm pregnant or am I in shock?

Doctor Anderson places a hand on my shoulder. Her fingers squeeze into the fabric of my gown. "I'm not kidding, Karen, you are pregnant."

I feel beads of sweat form on my forehead. My hands, already clammy, fly to my face in an attempt to hide the tears starting to pool in the corners of my eyes. I lunge forward, smack my toe on the stirrup again and scream. "This isn't possible. I'm forty-four years old." I try to shake her words from my head. Surely this dream will pop. I wrap my arms around my waist and lean forward. "How can I be pregnant at my age?"

Doctor Anderson slips gloves off her hands, smiles and pats my shoulder. "Well, you know Karen, it happens the same way it does when you are twenty."

I can't say her words make me feel less shocked. I also wonder if she thinks about the last time she told me I was pregnant.

Chapter Forty-Nine

My legs wobble when I leave the building. I scoot into the driver's seat of my car and let my head fall forward on to the steering wheel. Seems like crying is all I can do. I scrounge the front seat for tissues as my nose leaks like a faucet. I smack my hands hard on the center of the steering wheel and cause the horn to blare. This can't be.

How can this be possible? Where will we put a baby? Our friends will think we've lost our minds. My dad might suffer a heart attack when I tell him he'll be a grandparent again. My grown children will have a fit. The staff at the ranch will roll on the floor with laughter! Wasn't I just feeling good about losing those pebbles in my shoes?

I don't know how I manage to drive home without wrecking the car. I put the car into park but sit with the ignition on. How will I tell Jim? I continue to sit still when suddenly the next thought, which blitzes through my head, rips through my heart. Maybe I shouldn't have this baby? Oh gosh, did I just think that? Karen, what's wrong with you? Get it together!

I slowly open the front door to the house and peek inside. It's not quite lunchtime when Jim is usually home. Maybe it's better he's not here. I'm shaking. I'll just go on to the office. It's probably better for me to try to get a handle on this first before I see him.

Lois greets me. "Well, how did it go? I still hate going, even at my age. Oh, a few sales calls came in. I put the messages on your clip board." She turns to go back to her desk. I'm glad she doesn't wait for my answer.

I don't want my workday to end. I still don't believe I'm pregnant. When I close the office, and start to walk to the house, I see my dad walking down the lane. He must be coming back from Aunt Mary's house. I sure don't want to see him yet. I wave but continue my walk to our house.

Jim sits in his easy chair recliner in front of the television. I turn toward our bedroom door. "Hi honey, just putting my things away." By the time I enter our bedroom, once again I feel bile rise in my throat. I still question. Is this because I'm pregnant or scared? I quickly make a trip to the bathroom and empty my stomach. I stand, flush my face with cold water and look at my image in the mirror. Who is this woman in the mirror who even thought about abortion again? My hands fly to my sides to press on my abdomen. Get a grip Karen! I manage to freshen my face and dry my tears before I head to the family room.

Jim lumbers up from the couch. "How was your day, Hun?" He wraps his arms around me in the embrace I love to receive. I melt into his chest and bury my sobs into his neck. He pulls away just enough to look into my eyes. "Karen, what's wrong? Are you okay?" He holds my arms firmly. "What's wrong, honey?"

"Oh Jim, I don't know how to tell you." He draws me back into his arms. "Silly, you know you can tell me anything."

"I know, I know." I sniff. "I'm pregnant!"

I wait for Jim's response. He pulls me even closer into his chest. A low chuckle escapes from his lips and I feel his tears mingle with mine on my cheeks.

"Karen, this is so wonderful. Are you sure?"

I squeeze against him, but then I push away. "Yes." I turn my eyes toward the floor. "Yes, but, do you think I should have it at my age?"

I feel Jim stiffen, but then he scoops me up gently in his arms and walks to the couch. He sits down, still holding me tight in his arms. True to the honorable, God-loving man he is, he brushes tears from my eyes. "I think you know how I feel. I believe this baby is a gift from God we should honor. I also know how scary this may feel to you, but I'm sure the doctor would have told you if your age was a problem. I also know how you've struggled since you shared how you felt losing Jess's baby. Oh, Karen, God loves you. He has forgiven you." His arms tighten around me.

I feel a shudder tweak my spine… Why is the memory I confessed and thought I was free of sneaking into my heart? I haven't thought about that day since Jim and I married.

"Jim, I'm so sorry. You're right I'm just scared. I should have asked the doctor so many questions but I was overwhelmed. I dressed and left without going to her office for a consult."

Jim pulls me closer and touches the tip of my nose with his. "Let's call tomorrow and make an appointment to see her together. I feel certain she will take various tests. Hey woman, you are in great shape. This will be a piece of cake."

I snuggle close to him. "I love you so much. Thank you for being so understanding."

We talk for long hours into the night about what our lives might be like from this point forward. We talk about how we can turn the sunroom into a nursery. We question whether I should quit work and become a full-time mom again or ... we fall asleep in each other's arms. I dream about having a mass of pebbles, which have become rocks in my way.

The next morning Jim makes the coffee early. Every time he passes me, he pats my stomach. He can't stop smiling or touching me. Just before we kiss and say our farewells for the day, he leans in to my ear and whispers. "Now don't do anything stupid today. Don't lift anything heavy, please. We don't want to take any chances."

I don't need any further confirmation that Jim feels completely enthralled with the idea of parenthood. He even patted himself on the back this morning. He said, "Look at me, I still have the ammunition at forty-eight." Then he laughed all the way out of the room.

On the other hand, I feel shame gnaw its way back into my head for having thoughts of not having this baby.

I leave for work. As the day progresses, I realize this is an entirely different situation where I worry about our baby being healthy because of my age, not from any anger in my heart. At forty-four, a baby grows inside me. Three months, my doctor said. I make a vow to myself. I will not let a past memory of failure and sin push stones of any size in my way to play havoc with my happiness.

Chapter Fifty

On July 15, sharp pains riddle their way through my abdomen. At twenty-seven weeks' gestation, this certainly can't be labor. Isn't normal delivery thirty-five to forty something weeks? I try to move my body to a more comfortable position. Now, sharp pain stabs and twists inside me. I reach for the phone on the nightstand. I delivered my last child over twenty years ago. Now, at forty-four, I don't remember what labor should feel like. I call my doctor. She wants me to come to her office.

Jim has already left the house because one of the stallions is sick and he wants to be there when the vet arrives. I do my best between spasms of pain to put some clothes on and get to the car. I leave a note on the kitchen table just in case Jim gets back before I do, so he won't worry. I drive myself to the doctor's office.

She examines me. "You know Karen, I think we need to get you to the hospital just to be safe. We can put you on some meds to slow down or actually stop labor if this is what we are dealing with. She turns to remove her gloves and looks over her shoulder. So, do you think you can drive the block to the emergency room?"

I tell her I think I can, but when I get to my car, I realize something else is happening. I'm bleeding. By the time I arrive at the emergency room, my hands shake and my legs feel like jelly. Pain comes in spurts now, only minutes apart. I start to cry when a nurse meets me at the automatic doors of the ER. She rushes to place me in a wheelchair and takes me to a small labor room.

I spend a short time attached to machines monitoring my pain before Doctor Anderson informs me she wants to transfer me to a different hospital, which specializes in preemie births. My labor intensifies; the bleeding becomes more severe.

"Has anyone called my husband?"

"No, Karen, but we will do that now and we will have him go to the other hospital. We just need to have you sign a few papers before the transfer."

I've never ridden in an ambulance. I start to twist the ends of my hair. It's a real eerie feeling when I'm loaded in the back of the ambulance. Riding in an ambulance is downright scary!

Jim arrives at the hospital. I've only seen this kind of panic in his eyes when he didn't know how to tell me about my mother's death. He settles next to me in the labor room. He tells me how scared he felt when he received the call I'd been taken by ambulance to a hospital. He called his dad so he could let Lois know why I hadn't come to the office. Gentleness oozes from everything Jim says. His presence calms me.

A staff of nurses monitors my condition for the next two days. Jim never leaves my side. A doctor orders an ultrasound and while the technician performs the scan, she suddenly stops. "Excuse me, I need to get a doctor in here."

I look at Jim for his usual calm assurance. I watch his eyes narrow to slits. His jaw drops and quickly he brings it back up and clenches his teeth. I know that look. Jim is scared too.

A doctor burst through into the room with the technician at his heels. After he examines me, he pats my shoulder. "It looks like you're having your baby. I feel the baby's feet in the birth canal."

The technician pushes the gurney toward a delivery room. As she jogs down the hallway, Jim holds on to the IV stand and jogs right along with her. After another doctor examines me, he informs us that we have a little more time. A nurse wheels me back to the labor room.

In the labor area, only relatives can visit. I don't have any sisters but suddenly whole rafts of them sign the visitor list. A little red tape doesn't stop church family from getting in. Aunt Mary and Phyllis visit too. Their constant presence helps keep me sane my five days in labor. (I chuckle when I hear women complain about being in labor for ten or more hours.)

On July 18, a team of doctors enters the room. They explain to Jim and me, "If we can get corticosteroid into Karen for forty-eight hours, your baby's lungs can have a better chance of maturing." (Use of steroids reduces by half, the incidence of hyaline membrane disease. This occurs when the tiny air sacs collapse and stick together with every breath from lack of a substance known as surfactant, which provides surface tension in the lungs' air sacs.) We agree to the procedure.

On July 20, doctors need a decision. If they perform a Cesarean now, they can work in a controlled situation. Since it appears our baby wants to present herself early, this will be the safest route to take.

We face other problems because our baby's feet are emerging first with the umbilical cord ahead of them. One of the doctors comes in to talk to us.

"Karen and Jim, I must tell you we believe if the already strained water sac breaks, our situation might be critical. If this happens, I can't guarantee there won't be possible complications that might put your baby and you, Karen, in jeopardy. I'm obligated to explain that your baby, at twenty-seven weeks' gestation, might not survive."

The doctor puts his hand on Jim's shoulder. "We'll be ready shortly. Someone will be in soon to wheel Karen to the OR."

Jim's faith never seems to waiver. "God's in charge, Karen. He's going to take care of everything."

I wish I felt positive. My trust dissolves right then and there. My thoughts quickly go to a statement I made over and over after Jess and Mom died. Why is God letting this happen? Why now, is He going to slip boulders in my shoes?

Soft music plays on an intercom in the delivery room. I guess this is supposed to soothe patients. It doesn't work for me! Dread pricks every nerve in my body. Jim sits on a stool close behind me with his hand on my shoulder. The brightly lit room, so cold, stark and sterile offers me zero comfort.

An anesthesiologist numbs me from the waist down by inserting a needle, filled with a drug for the job, into my spine. Since I remain awake as my lower body starts to feel like it doesn't belong to me anymore, I look around at my surroundings. On the left side of the room, I watch one nurse fiddle with wires and machines attached to an incubator.

Another, standing close behind her, appears to give her instructions in a whispered voice. The third nurse takes a position beside one of the doctors. She lifts her gloved hands above her chest and nods. Keeping his voice light and cheery, my neonatal doctor says, "I think we are ready Karen. We're going to give you a slight sedative to relax you, but you will still be awake."

My hands clutch the sides of the table so hard that the muscles in my forearms hurt. Within minutes after he administers medicine in my IV, my tense arms fall limp on the gurney and I lie still, in an almost who cares state of mind.

Jim lowers his head, closer to mine. His fingers stroke my face. Gently he pushes wisps of my bangs from my eyes and lays his head against mine. I think we both know we don't have any control over what is about to take place, but I do know we pray. Jim prays out loud, so loudly, I think the doctors might throw him out of the OR.

Chapter Fifty-One

My doctor says, "Here we go Karen." It feels eerie because I can't feel anything; but I hope he has a steady hand, because I know he holds a knife to draw an incision across my lower abdomen and soon our little girl will appear.

Jim prays more loudly. "God please bring our baby girl into our crazy world safe. Please give her a will to survive the odds against her."

Suddenly Jim's fingers grip my shoulder with a force, which makes me squeeze my eyes shut. He whispers in my ear. "Karen, I can hardly breathe. There's a rainbow of color all around you and the room is so warm. Do you feel it?" The urgency I hear in his voice scares me.

"What do you mean?" My own voice sounds equally strange as I try to reach for Jim's hand.

"I don't know, Karen."

Fervently he prays even louder, "Please help us God. I'm so scared. Please let Karen and our baby live. Show me some sign you're here. We need you."

His eyes open wide. "Karen, something crazy is happening. I know I'm sounding nuts, but... can you feel it? I'm not kidding."

Jim scares me. I try to concentrate on the doctor's voice as he explains the C-Section procedure. Jim continues to whisper in my ear. "Someone is touching my chest, Karen, pushing on it." I watch Jim move backward. Confused, I look at the doctors but no one seems to pay attention. Tears flood Jim's cheeks. He slumps forward.

The volume on the intercom playing the soft music becomes loud. Stevie Wonder sings, "I Just Called To Say I Love You." It takes a few seconds for Jim and me to realize our special song, one we listen to over and over almost every day, has just started to play on the intercom. The doctors' heads pop up briefly. They seem to notice the volume change in the intercom. I think they look a little startled before they turn their heads back toward the task at hand.

I see one doctor raise something in his hands. My head whips forward off the flat gurney. Suddenly, all three nurses crowd close to me. "We have a girl," the doctor announces. Before his words settle into my fogged mind, the room explodes with activity.

All three nurses become energized and scurry to the left side of the room. One of them carries our baby girl. She carries her with one hand. The entire scene seems surreal to me. Tears spill down my face. My arms still feel heavy. I can't lift them in order to wipe my tears. I look at Jim. His eyes sparkle from his own tears but a smile stretches across his face.

Jim's sudden intake of breath startles me. When he releases it, his head drops into the nape of my neck. He starts to sob. He feathers a kiss on my forehead and says, "Karen, did you hear that? God just called to say He loves us. He's right here."

As our song trails off to its end... "And I mean it from the bottom of my heart." I lay my head back until it falls into the crook of Jim's arm and I let my eyes focus on the ceiling. My heart thumps in my chest but my mind plays the scene over in my head. I pray quietly, "Thank you God, thank you for your grace and mercy."

Jim is so right. How can it be a coincidence, that at the very moment the doctor delivers our premature baby, our song comes blaring on the intercom?

How else can Jim's vision of soft rainbow colors around me just before her birth and the pressure of a hand on his chest as he prayed out loud be explained? No one will ever convince Jim God didn't place His hand on his chest to assure him of His presence.

I've come to understand since my talk with Pastor David, that now when I am thrown into a situation beyond my control,

I'm helpless unless I look to a higher power than my own.

I've relived my disobedience to God throughout much of my life, but at this moment, I believe God is never limited by human failure or my sins. I believe He works through ordinary people like Jim and me. Truly I feel, as I look into Jim's eyes, a miracle just took place.

Chapter Fifty-Two

After the delivery, Phyllis, Jenny and Aunt Mary join us in the recovery room. As they hold my hands, I wonder if they realize I just delivered a baby girl almost three months early? I don't believe it myself. I search their expressions. Up to this point, I think our friends and family didn't really comprehend the fact we were going to be parents. The reality of what Jim and I might face starts to sink into my head. These thoughts blur my happiness. Is our baby going to live? I didn't hear her cry...is she alive?

After a short stint in recovery, a nurse wheels me to a room to get me settled. "We're going to take your vitals, Karen, then someone will take you and your husband to see your baby, once she is stabilized." I want to ask her, when can I hold her? Does she have all her fingers and toes?

It seems like an eternity before a nurse walks back into the room and asks Jim and me if we are ready to see our baby.

When she pushes a button to open the swinging doors of the Neonatal Intensive

Care Unit, several large stainless sinks line the wall in front of us. We wash our hands and arms, all the way to our elbows, with antiseptic orange soap. We each don pale blue gowns and place a facemask over our noses and mouths. I don't know if the pain I feel comes from having a C-section or because I don't know what lies behind the next set of swinging doors.

Blinking lights immediately attack my senses. People scurry around like ants. A maze of machines, wires, hoses and blaring alarms accost me. I want to get past all the technology in the room. I just want to focus on my baby. I think Jim feels my anxiety. He reaches out and grabs my hand. Doctors and nurses clutter around incubators. Every face I look at appears serious and downright sad. I don't see any smiles, mainly pursed lips or wrinkled foreheads.

The nurse pushes the wheelchair to a stop in front of an incubator. A sign reads, "Baby G." I fold my hands across my chest when I see our baby. A wail of shock creeps up from my throat. It spills out as I look at her through the glass of the incubator... No way is 'this' going to live. Wires and tubes pierce all parts of her minute torso. Jaundiced, her eerie yellow skin against the white sheet makes me look away and catch my breath. She glows under phototherapy lights.

A tiny blindfold covers her eyes. I ask Jim to push me closer so I can examine her. Nothing about her looks real. Her transparent skin makes her blue veins stand out. They resemble roads in a map veering through her body. Only eleven inches long, she now weighs one pound nine ounces. Her bird-like legs twitch. I long to touch her tiny fingers. They are no longer than a red sulfur tip on a wooden kitchen match.

I want to hold her close to my chest and protect her. No longer do silent tears fall. "No, no," I sob. The patient and kind staff try to console me. I am inconsolable.

After a few minutes the soothing voice of the nurse attending our baby uses her strong hands to massage my shoulders. My sobs lessen. "It's okay, Karen. Go ahead and cry. We are going to take very good care of your baby, but we need you … she needs you to be strong." I take a deep breath. God really knows what He's doing when He places these souls into this line of work.

***

In the days that follow, Jim and I cherish every affirmation of our baby's fight for survival. Responses from her, the opening of her eyes or what we imagine is a possible smile on her lips produce emotional peaks of joy for us. My hope is to believe positive days will compensate for the many valleys of despair I see in front of us.

We ask our nurse questions about the wires and machines. She explains to us, "a preemie's nervous system is not developed, so your baby can't shiver or sweat. We need to attach sensors to assure us that she is neither too hot nor too cold. If this isn't monitored, your baby might burn up calories she can't afford to lose."

Our nurse smiles before she reaches her hands through the two holes in the side of the incubator. "Preemies are born without subcutaneous fat, which is the thermal layer directly under the skin. It controls a baby's temperature."

Then she points to the tiny circles on our baby's chest. "This alarm monitors apnea. Apnea occurs when a baby forgets to breathe. If these go undetected, the heart rate can slow down. This is called Bradycardia. It can cause sudden death."

I'm starting to freak out. I'm glad I'm sitting in a wheelchair. While my own tears fall, I ask why our baby doesn't cry. Our nurse explains that a preemie's cry can't be heard when they have a tube in their mouth. Later, when the tube comes out, our baby's throat may be so sore that crying is too painful. I try to imagine what this must feel like. I swallow. My own throat constricts. I want all my baby's pain to be given to me. Goose bumps rise in little pimples on my arms. Please, God, help her.

One doctor tells us, "Once treatment for each individual child begins, there are no guarantees, only probabilities. Even babies who do well can suddenly take a turn for the worse. It's like an obstacle course; over one hurdle but no telling if even bigger hurdles lie ahead." His honesty scares me to death. Do I really need all this negative information?

Once I allow his message to settle in my brain, I guess this information does help me understand how preemies struggle to survive, grow and develop; but it doesn't make me feel any better. I wonder how long it might take me to get used to the wires and tubes, to understand they help form our baby's 'substitute womb.' Trust me, this seems like an impossible task. Right now, I feel there's another avalanche of boulders in my way.

Chapter Fifty-Three

For the first few weeks, our baby wears a surgical mask, two sizes too big, for a diaper. Debee sends us a package full of preemie Cabbage Patch doll clothes. The sleeves and legs of the clothes need to be rolled up several inches in order to come close to fitting.

Every day we face a new hurdle, some with feelings of futility; others with humor. A favorite nurse tells us, "A preemie is an organism in an environment he has not yet evolved for." She also places a sign above our baby's incubator. It reads: "Please be patient. God hasn't finished me yet."

Our baby suffers a brain hemorrhage a few days after her birth. The doctor on duty assures us this is a common occurrence in preemie births, but I imagine mental disabilities, surgery or special needs. These images run rampant in front of my eyes. Later in the week a doctor explains the hemorrhage might have happened in utero. Does he think this news makes me feel better?

Another day passes and our baby needs a transfusion. I actually get down on my hands and knees to beg a doctor to let me donate blood for the transfusion. At first, he says I might be too weak from having a C-Section. I'd like to say he gives in but I demand he use my blood.

I sit next to the incubator. I watch as, drip by drip, my blood filters into her tiny vein. During times like this, prayer is the only sound from my lips. I must tell a truth here though; I don't feel a connection with God. I pray, but I often feel void of emotion.

Jim's faith, on the other hand, stays strong. I become angry with him when he talks about God's will and how everything will be okay. Trust, he keeps repeating. I tell him, "You don't care about our baby as much as I do or else you would worry too."

After several more weeks' pass, we bring our baby out of the incubator into real air for just a few minutes each day. I remind myself daily that preemie babies are required at birth to accomplish the amazing feat of breathing room air. Their tiny little lungs are immature. When I can finally hold her close to my chest, I'm shocked because I feel like I have nothing in my arms. The nurse has me open the buttons on my blouse so I can place our baby on my bare chest. This is when I lose all my composure. I can actually hold her entire body with one hand. The nurse rearranges the wires away from my skin when the alarm on the heart monitor starts to squeal. Every nerve in my body begins to quiver and tense with fear.

"What's wrong? Is she okay? What should I do?"

The nurse steps toward me, "You're okay Karen. Your baby is fine. She stopped breathing for just a second. She's fine. Just keep her against your chest. There ... you're doing great. When this happens, Karen, all you have to do is massage her chest gently to bring her breath back." She places two fingers on our baby's chest and moves them in a circular motion. The alarm stops.

Doctors tell us breastfeeding is best for our preemie. This hurts me deeply because, since my cancer surgery, I'm unable to do this. Nurses assure me our baby will do just fine on formula. Surely others have faced this. The first time I witness a nurse feed our baby through a tube and line in her nose, I nearly pass out. Now this week I'm thrilled to hold the tube and feed her myself. The procedure is called gavage feeding.

Do I believe God watches over us on our journey so far? Not entirely. Every day I find myself giving God lots of lip service. I pray for strength for myself. I pray for our baby to live. I'm not exactly giving praise or thanks for all the positive things that are happening.

Right now, I struggle with trust. I'm supposed to put all of this in God's hands but all I see are my own struggles. I feel awful Jim has to put up with my mood swings and my inability to surrender this trial to God. I'm angry with God again! What is wrong with me?

My trust in God's plan is put to another test when it's time for me to leave the hospital. I'm going home without my baby. I feel the pebbles in my way under my paper slippers.

Chapter Fifty-Four

When I leave the hospital without my baby, my anger and frustration stifles every positive thought I try to muster. I feel deprived and scared. It isn't normal for a mother to leave her newborn baby behind in the arms of strangers.

I have a huge support system; Jim, family and friends, but I feel alone. Only the big bouquets of flowers lining the backseat of our truck when we drive away, and the pain from my C-Section, remind me I've delivered a baby. Don't let anyone tell you it's easy to have a Cesarean at forty-four like it might be at twenty.

Some of our church friends suggest I'll get a lot of rest because I don't have to care for our baby while she stays in the hospital but I go back to work because the hospital bills are outrageous. Mr. Green gives me time off throughout my workday to make afternoon trips to the hospital. Jim and I drive to and from the hospital in the evenings together. I don't feel rested!

We try our best to bond through the incubator glass by putting our hands through two small holes in the side. When we hold her, we feel awkward as we coo and sing to her. It feels so unnatural because so many doctors, nurses and other families with babies in the same situation, rush around us.

This evening we come to the hospital excited because we have finally decided on a name. We call her Grace. It just seems like a perfect name for her since Jim feels so strongly that God's grace is the reason she lives. I love the name but I still question the why of her early birth. Every second I think about Grace, my lips form the words; please watch over her God. In the back of my mind I question if I'm praying right, or enough. There I go again. Why can't I just trust?

Slowly Grace begins to open her eyes for longer periods of time. Occasionally we hear a faint cry; still more like a squeak. We bring her out of the incubator into the real air for longer periods of time. Little by little, nurses remove more wires and tubes from her tiny torso. I constantly have to remind myself that preemies are not expected to act like full term babies.

I think adrenaline keeps me going. I start to understand, first hand, how fragile life really is. I desperately want to be a mother to this child. I often feel hopeless.

Several babies die during our Grace's stay in the NICU. When I listen to the wails of a mother who loses a child, my own fear of losing mine quadruples. When this happens, I want to curl up into a ball and scream.

Prayers continue from many sources. Aunt Mary and Phyllis place us on many prayer lists. Nurses confide in us that they pray for our family daily. In spite of constant reassurance of prayer vigils, I'll admit once again, my trust in the Lord, based on no real understanding of commitment to Him during this trial, still shatters easily.

Jim encourages me daily. He insists everything is in God's hands. He tells me God wants Grace in the world for a purpose. I still feel since Jim doesn't seem worried, he must not care about Grace as much as I do. I wonder how long before I'll start to feel secure. Maybe Jim is right. He keeps saying God has a plan for us. I just want God to reveal it now, right now.

***

When our pediatrician, who drives from across town to see our Grace daily, informs us he wants to move her to our local hospital in Scottsdale because he believes the smaller hospital can give her closer attention, I begin to feel more hopeful. Also, if an emergency arises, his office is only blocks away. Encouraged our Grace is ready for a move, I ask God to help us make a smooth transition.

We gather the family in the evening and tell them what the next step is. Dad and Aunt Mary show animated glee by joining hands and dancing around the family room. Mr. Green, Phyllis and Kent, all who visit the hospital every day are just as thrilled. Everyone offers encouragement.

I still feel overwhelmed. The phone rings and when Jim answers it, he tells me it's my grown kids checking in. It's been almost two months now since Grace's birth. My grown kids haven't been able to get away to make a trip to see her. They tell me how excited they are to hear Grace is doing so well. My daughter is quick to tell me she is doing research and is sure little Grace is going to be home soon and she will grow up strong. Old teary me has a breakdown and Jim has to retrieve the phone and finish the conversation.

***

I dress Grace in her prettiest pink doll dress, one with lace forming the hem. The attending nurse tapes a pink bow on top of her head. Jim and I drive ahead of the ambulance transporting her to Scottsdale.

From a 64-bed unit, we are now in a small room with one other preemie and four full time nurses. We become a real family over the next month.

Our tiny miracle baby starts to thrive. Nurses remove most of the tubes and wires. She still wears two white circular patches with wires attached to the heart monitor. Every day, her skin takes on a pinker hue. The fine hair covering her body has disappeared. Her eyes look so big in her little face that when her sister finally meets her she says, "She looks like E.T."

After my daughter's surprise visit, I treasure the blessing for me to have her support in the early stage of her little sister's beginning. Then on Labor Day weekend, while I feed Grace, I look up to see my son peek through the nursery window. I squeal with delight as I place his tiny sister in his arms for the first time. Standing at six foot two, he looks somewhat unsure as he brings her to his chest. She looks especially tiny in her big brother's arms. I hold back my tears because I know he and his sister are well on their own journeys in life and I'm sad they might not get a chance to play a bigger part in Grace's life.

***

At the end of a day I'm completely drained of energy, physically and emotionally. I'm grateful my job keeps my mind busy between hospital runs. Mr. Green keeps my hours flexible. It doesn't hurt that he's my father-in-law. He also gave Jim and me financial assistance when we moved Grace to the new hospital. Later, he gifted the loan to us. Fathers-in-law are like this you know.

More and more positive days in our journey start to encourage my faith in God's part in all of this. It's not that I think if fewer things go smoothly, God doesn't care. I know we still have many hurdles to get through and I expect some of them will be difficult. I think it's only a normal reaction when positive things happen, faith seems to increase.

Chapter Fifty-Five

Finally, the big day arrives. Our pediatrician announces we can take Grace home. We don't believe it. She only weighs three pounds fourteen ounces. I thought babies had to weigh at least five pounds before they can go home. Our doctor tries to soothe my fears. He says, "Your baby is eating, sleeping, drinking and going to the bathroom. She is just little. She is ready."

Jim and I rush to shop for preemie diapers, bottles and a multitude of items we need for Grace's homecoming. I truly believe I didn't think she would ever come home. Not only that but by our count we still had thirteen weeks of pregnancy to go! We are certainly not prepared.

The nurses enroll us in special CPR classes for preemie babies. They give us instructions on the heart monitor. Grace will be attached to it for the next ten months. The alarm on the monitor will tell us when she stops breathing so we can stimulate her chest. We are given a prescription for caffeine to place into her formula daily to stimulate her heart. We joke she might become a Starbucks junkie. This tickles Jim because everyone knows how much he loves his coffee.

The hospital has a special program for mothers of preemies. As a preparation for taking Grace home, I can spend a few nights in a room at the hospital. With the comfort of knowing nurses are close by, Grace and I can have a chance to bond alone. I jump at the chance. This will also give Jim a chance to put the crib together and buy more supplies.

***

Tonight's the first night. I'll admit I'm really nervous. When the nurse brings Grace to me, she hands me formula, diapers and lots of encouragement. Then … she shuts the door. Alone at last with my Grace, I sit on the edge of the bed and watch her chest rise and fall. Several times the heart monitor blares. Even though I've heard the alarm many times before, I can't shake a feeling of dread something more might be wrong with her. I reach across the open incubator and gently massage her tiny chest to help her breathe.

I gingerly reach into the side of her diaper to see if she needs changed. I feel a slight dampness but don't want to wake her from her sound sleep. She starts to whimper a few minutes later. I know she must be hungry because it's been almost two hours since the nurses brought her to me. I fumble with her formula. Her cry becomes more intense. She now has a pair of lungs capable of letting me know she is really angry. I carefully pick her up and cradle her in my arms. Her little mouth grabs on to the nipple so forcefully it surprises me. This routine continues every two hours. I don't sleep.

I open the drawer on the nightstand next to my bed. A small black Bible beckons me. I must say, my first thought is, oh great, where are the magazines. I pick up the Bible. I start to thumb through the pages when it slips out of my hands and falls open on the bed.

"Put off your old self, which belongs to your former manner of life and is corrupt though deceitful desires...be renewed in the spirit of your mind and put on the new self, created after the likeness of God in true righteousness and holiness." I feel like someone just threw cold water in my face... my new self? How am I new?

Uncontrollable torrents of tears race down my cheeks. Immediately I think about the life I feel I ended. The person I used to be so long ago flashes before me. My chest tightens. I remember my humble confession with Pastor Rodney and then Pastor David only recently. Have I changed? Did I give up my old self? Do I feel Jesus' presence? Do I just pray for what I want? Pastor Rodney's words, lip service, ring in my ears.

Almost frantically I finger through the pages of the Bible. It's as if the Bible turns its own pages. Even though I've read through a Bible before, certain scripture seems to appear before me on its own accord.

"I rejoice not because you were grieved into repenting, for you felt a godly grief, so that you suffered no loss through us. For Godly grief produces a repentance that leads to salvation without regret, whereas worldly grief produces death. For see what earnestness this godly grief has produced in you, but also what eagerness to clear yourselves, what indignation, what fear, what longing, what zeal, what punishment. At every point, you have proved yourselves innocent in the matter."

I cover my face with my hands. My body trembles. I peek through my fingers to read the passage again. Why is this happening to me? For the rest of the night, between feedings, I read more and more scripture in this incredible book and realize I've put it aside for far too long.

Right here in front of me, I realize once again, the words I read, convict me and at the same time comfort me. Have I not been listening when Jim reads Bible verses out loud before bedtime? Is it just normal to be a believer but have all the fears I have? Have I really given up my old self?

I really thought I had committed myself to my Savior after speaking to Pastor David. I shared my entire life with him and since he married us, Jim and I have attended church regularly. I also know I've been unable to put my past completely out of my mind. Not because I was such an evil person, but maybe because I've not consciously taken a new life in Christ seriously.

Grace is still sleeping, so I take a few more minutes to reflect on my past life, way before Jess or Jim, one I'd led with an entirely different set of values. Why, now, do the words in front of me cause such a powerful reaction? Why am I reliving so many years past?

For some reason, as I sit here on the edge of a hospital bed and gaze at my little miracle, I realize for the first time that I, self, need to throw up my hands and surrender more than just my confessed sins. Lip service needs to be replaced with a commitment to understand what God really wants from me. Has He given me a second chance? Does He want me to stop looking for the pebbles my way?

Isn't commitment an agreement or pledge to do something in a state of being obligated or emotionally impelled to a cause? Pastor David often speaks of how God talks to us if we become silent enough to listen. I suddenly feel goose bumps pepper my arms. Maybe this miracle, this second chance God has given me, is His ultimate thump on my head to make me let go and quit feeling like pebbles, rocks or boulders control me!

Yep, God really needs more than lip service from me. This must be one of those 'aha moments' I've heard about where people understand God wants commitment from our heart. I need to attend to His desires. I take in a deep breath of air.

I look at my tiny bundle asleep in front of me. I think it might be this moment I believe I can equal the care for Grace, which three different nurses presently supply. I actually don't feel inadequate.

Is it a fluke I open a drawer in a hospital room to discover a Bible, which seems to open by its self? I don't think so. Perhaps God gave me Grace as a kind of second chance. Then maybe He decided an early preemie birth would be the trial I need to fully understand how precious and fragile a life is. Maybe, He needs me to understand and treasure this life He gave me at forty-four years of age. Yes, He has forgiven a heinous sin in my life, but maybe He feels I need a constant nudge to remember my disobedience. A deep sigh escapes from my lips. I'm feeling almost giddy. I think God is truly giving me a chance to right a wrong and clear the annoyances, no matter what size from my path forever.

When the nurse comes to my room in the morning I feel like a zombie. I eagerly hand Grace to her. Two more nights in the hospital give me a sense of security I might be ready to take her home.

Tomorrow is the big day. We get to bring Grace home.

Chapter Fifty-Six

I love the Green family. Most of the tribe comes in separate cars to the hospital this morning to bring Grace home. Jim tucks an infant car seat in the backseat of our car with several towels padding the insides. The nurses told us to do this because Grace will still be too tiny for a car seat.

Our favorite nurse dresses little Grace in a girly pink outfit and packs a small bag full of supplies as a going away gift.

Everyone's eyes sparkle with moisture. I'm only a tad bit scared to think we are now going to be on our own. I've already turned forty-five and still question my abilities to mother again. Jim puffs out his chest like a gorilla and seems to have complete confidence in our parenting skills. I laugh. What does he know? This is his first!

All the way home, I turn my body toward the back seat to watch Grace's chest rise and fall. She sleeps. As we make our way home and turn down our tree-lined lane, I can't believe what I see. Someone has tied pink balloons to all the trees. They blow and flutter in a soft breeze. It's comical to see the mares in the field because they have moved as far away from the lane as possible because of the balloons.

"Oh, Jim, do you know who did this?" I place my hand on my chest and stare in awe.

"I bet we can blame your Aunt Mary. When we left to come to the hospital, she said she needed to stay home to take care of a few things. Yep, bet it was good 'ole Aunt Mary. I just hope your dad isn't the one who used a ladder." Jim lays his hand hard on the horn when we see Dad and Aunt Mary waving to us from the end of the lane.

I can almost end my story right here. After all, it feels like a happily ever after. But, I want to share a few more thoughts.

Has God worked hard to save me? I think He worked overtime all these years. His voice lingered in my head since childhood. Most of my young adult life I chose not to listen. I've learned believing in God is not enough. I need to have a daily relationship with Him. If I'm not practicing living His commands, His way of life for me, then I'm not living the life His words ask me to live.

Some people believe when bad things happen to them, God is punishing them for a wrong they've done. I think this might be possible, but I believe the bad things are caused, most of the time, from our own free will, the choices we make and our humanness to be self-absorbed. I don't know if I'd be the person I am today, coming home to this joyful reception, if the many wrong choices I made hadn't taught me so much about myself. Each lesson pushed me closer and closer into God's arms. Sometimes I fought Him all the way.

I also see now how only God could have brought me through some of the trials I faced in my younger years. I've experienced as I've grown older a closed door often brings an arcadia type one which can bring new joy. Over time and often, I've learned something good is eventually learned from tragedy and trial.

God brought me Jess. He placed him in my life because God knew he possessed a conviction to live a God-centered life. I lost Jess and yes something good did come from a trial I thought would destroy me. God brought me Jim. I lost my mom, but God placed Aunt Mary in my path. I lost Ibn and God put Miss Diamond in my life. I can go on and on.

***

Sitting here in Jim's grandmother's rocker, I hold Grace in my arms and think about my encounter with a Bible in the hospital. Since we've been home, I try to lay all my challenges at the Lord's feet. I look back now and know, before I gave birth to Grace, she and I must have been secured in a complex dance. After her birth, a hospital provided an artificial womb, but a hospital doesn't produce feelings and hope I intricately feel with my child. I believe only God does this.

Sometimes the great responsibility of being a part of Christ's family scares me. I have to remember; Christ promises me great reward if I follow Him. He also shows me through scripture I will encounter constant trials on earth.

I wasted much of my life on self-absorption and lip service. Scripture says, "We cannot serve self and our Lord at the same time." I'm exhilarated today because I know my past is forgotten and new options await me every day. The painful lessons I'll still experience may even open doorways to better opportunities. I'm starting to smile when I'm forced to look forward instead of inward.

The hardest thing for me to do still, is to sing praise the moment a trial appears. I think when God tests my faith He helps me develop perseverance. "But we also rejoice in our sufferings; because we know that suffering produces perseverance, perseverance produces character and character, hope." As hard as it is to be tested, eternity IS my hope.

Does this sound like I'm complete in some sort of victory over pain, sadness or fear? Of course not! I will 'fall out' of God's grace because of my humanness. I'm sure I will contradict God's word often during the rest of my life, because I understand how hard it is to not cling to the world and its values. The Lord caught me in His out-stretched hands more often than not. How lucky am I, He gives His grace free to believers. I've started to understand how God picks me up over and over so I can walk with Him.

My story, my experience is almost complete on paper. I've journeyed through my mid-life season with a twist on late pregnancy. I'm certain many people struggle with more difficult, painful or downright scary trials, but I can only share my belief. There is hope if Christ is a partner in life and self is monitored carefully.

Yes, I think I will end my story here and I'm going to put the pebbles in God's hands.

Jim walks to the rocker and kisses the top of my head. He brushes his fingers across Grace's tiny cheek. I bring her to my shoulder, all three and a half pounds of her. Swaddled in my arms, she reminds me of God's faithfulness. Happy endings always feel good.

—*About Alice Klies*—

Alice has written since she could hold a pencil. She is currently president of Northern Arizona Word Weavers, a chapter of an international writers group. It is through their encouragement Alice began to submit her work for publication. She has nonfiction and fiction stories published in sixteen anthologies. She is a seven-time contributor to Chicken Soup For The Soul books and has articles published in Angels On Earth, AARP and Wordsmith Journal. She has also been featured in the Women of Distinction magazine. Besides her involvement in Word Weavers, she serves on boards for the PWG (Professional Women's Group) and Y.E.S. the ARC in her community. She is a deaconess and Stephens Minister in her church.

Alice is a retired teacher who resides with her husband and two Golden Retrievers in beautiful Cottonwood, Arizona. She prays her stories cause a reader to smile, laugh or cry, and most of all turn their eyes upward to God who loves them.

53514323R00191

Made in the USA
San Bernardino, CA
19 September 2017